ELIMINATING SELF-DEFEATING BEHAVIORS SYSTEM

James E. Cerio, Ph.D.

Psychologist
Associate Professor, Counseling and Psychology
Harford Community College

James F. LaCalle, Ed.D.

Associate Dean, Continuing Education Division
Harford Community College

James P. Murtha, Ph.D.

Associate Dean, Human Development Division
Harford Community College

ACCELERATED DEVELOPMENT INC.

Publishers

Muncie,   Indiana

ELIMINATING SELF-DEFEATING BEHAVIORS SYSTEM

Library of Congress Number: 86-71217

International Standard Book Number: 0-915202-60-3

Technical Development: Tanya Dalton
Judy McWilliams
Sheila Sheward

Cover Design: Ralph Jordan
T/A Confluence Associates
Havre de Grace, MD 21078

AD ACCELERATED DEVELOPMENT INC., PUBLISHERS
3400 Kilgore Avenue, Muncie, IN 47304
(317) 284-7511

DEDICATION

To those who have participated in our workshops,
for their contributions to the development of the concepts in this book.

FOREWORD

Most readers can profit from reading this book and completing its exercises—especially when they can read and discuss it with a trusted friend or relative. It teaches readers that they have learned to be what they are and that they can learn productive new behaviors to replace their self-defeating ones. It helps them to recognize their own self-defeating behaviors, to explore why they persist, to understand precisely how these behaviors interfere with achievement of desired goals, and to decide precisely what new behaviors they must learn to replace their self-defeating ones.

On the other hand, this book can be used much more effectively by a competent counselor in a counseling group, and also effectively by a counselor in personal growth groups, classroom discussions, and workshops. Fellow participants are quick to see through one anothers' unproductive games. Fellow participants also provide encouragement, support, and reinforcement.

Finally, this book gives readers hope. They can change. They do not have to continue to believe that they are victims. Each can learn to take charge and manage his/her life.

This book is well written. The examples make sense, and the exercises should be very helpful.

Merle M. Ohlsen, Ph.D.
Registered Psychologist, Illinois
Champaign, Illinois

Holmstedt Distinguished Professor
    Emeritus of Guidance and
    Psychological Services
Indiana State University

Professor Emeritus of Educational
    Psychology
University of Illinois

PREFACE

Cognitive-behavioral approaches are among the most popular counseling approaches in use today. Their attention to the thoughts, actions, and feelings of people who engage in productive and problematic behaviors has contributed to their popularity. They help to explain most behaviors as well as provide procedures for overcoming self-defeating behaviors. Cognitive-behavioral approaches are the foundation of this book.

Development of this book began three years ago when we formulated a packet of material from previous handouts used in our Eliminating Self-Defeating Behaviors workshops at Harford Community College and Essex Community College. Since then, several revisions have occurred, thanks to the recommendations of counseling clients, workshop participants, and Dr. Joseph Hollis of Accelerated Development Inc. We are finding that revisions are occurring even as the manuscript is going to press. Part of the excitement of working with this material is finding more ways for it to be presented and applied almost every time that it is used.

In Unit One, several uses for this book are described. The model, developed by Dr. Nancy Stockton, is presented in Unit Two. In Units Three, Four, and Five are offered several strategies for eliminating self-defeating behaviors. These strategies are organized according to their principal target—thoughts, actions, and feelings. In Unit Six the suggestion is made that these same strategies can be used to achieve self-enhancing behaviors.

We wish to acknowledge and thank Dr. Nancy Stockton, psychologist, at Counseling and Psychological Services, Student Health Service, Indiana University in Bloomington, Indiana. Nancy created the workshop "Elimination of Self-Defeating Behaviors" at Indiana University in the mid-1970s. Much of the material in this book is based upon her work.

We hope that this book will help readers explain their behavior and behave more productively. For these purposes this book was written.

JEC, JFL, JPM
Bel Air, Maryland
June 8, 1986

CONTENT

ACTIVITIES

Eliminating Self-Defeating Behaviors System

UNIT **ONE**

HOW TO USE THIS BOOK

"How can I get the most out of this book?"

This book will help people who have decided that the time has come to eliminate behaviors that are irrational, unproductive, and self-defeating. As you proceed through this book, you will read about some of the negative aspects of human behavior. However, realize that positive, self-enhancing behavior is common, even in people who tend to perceive their behavior in a negative manner. Contrary to what some people may believe, a psychologically healthy and happy life is not overly difficult to achieve.

Some of the characteristics of a psychologically healthy person are flexibility, spontaneity, and creativity. Such people are generally free from tension and anxiety, are able to cope with problems that confront them, possess a sense of humor that is not hostile, are able to laugh at themselves, and have a capacity for playfulness. In addition, emotionally healthy people find it relatively easy to relate to others and have the capacity for intimate, loving relationships. One of the most important characteristics of healthy individuals is their ability to see themselves and the world around them in a realistic manner. The ability to perceive reality accurately is an important indicator of good mental health.

In spite of the desire to behave "normally," people often behave in ways that keep them from leading happy lives. Rather than being positive and realistic, people allow their thoughts, actions, and feelings to combine in complex ways to create behaviors which cause problems in daily living. These behaviors are not caused by other people; each individual alone is responsible for his/her behaviors.

While many reasons exist for people engaging in unhealthy and self-defeating behaviors, eliminating even undesirable behaviors can be a difficult task. Behavioral change is not always possible in all areas of life due to heredity or strong early environmental forces. Habit, attitudes, and opinions may deter change and growth because they reduce receptiveness to alternative ways of thinking and acting. Defensive behavior patterns can deter change and growth by providing mechanisms for the distortion of reality.

However, all is not lost! In spite of most people's inherent resistance to change, personal growth may be achieved by developing attitudes and behaviors that are marked by openness, receptivity to new experience, curiosity, eagerness, lack of fear, and experimentality.

Purposes of This Book

The *purposes of this book, therefore, are to help you view your behavior in a more objective fashion, teach you to recognize your own particular ways of resisting change, and illustrate techniques of substituting desirable for undesirable behavior.* Keep in mind that although change can be difficult, people generally have more ability and potential for change and personal growth than they credit to themselves.

The *primary objective of this book is to help you learn a strategy for eliminating your self-defeating behaviors.* As you attempt to achieve this "master objective," several, more specific, objectives also will be accomplished along the way. Specifically, you will begin to understand the reasons why you behave as you do, learn some terms and concepts commonly used in the field of psychology, develop a working knowledge of the Eliminating Self-Defeating Behaviors (ESDB) System, apply the ESDB System to your own self-defeating behaviors, and learn how to become a more "fully-functioning" person.

We should mention, however, that the ESDB System has some limitations. For example, it is not designed to overcome serious emotional or behavioral problems, nor can it "change your personality" to any significant degree. Rather, by use of this book you will learn to change specific behaviors. Finally, this book is designed to help you, not "someone else." That is, if another person in your life is one whom you think needs help with a problem, the responsibility to do something about it is that person's, not yours. You cannot do someone else's "job" for him/her, however well intended you may be. You can offer support and assistance but the responsibility belongs to the other person.

Uses of This Book

This book is written in a way that allows the reader to move logically through a complete system for eliminating self-defeating behaviors. The best way to use this book, consequently, is to read the text and attempt the activities from Units Two through Six in the order in which they are presented.

Throughout each unit sample activities are presented. These are activities "completed" by two fictitious people—Kathy and Mike—who have tried to eliminate their SDBs by using this book. These sample activities, which follow each activity that the reader is to complete, are presented as models or examples for anyone needing help while working through this book. The samples thus help the reader understand how to use the ESDB System. Anyone using this book should then be able to apply the activities to his/her unique situation.

This book could be used by (1) an individual, (2) participants in an ESDB Workshop, (3) students in a class wanting to eliminate self-defeating behaviors while studying related material, (4) counselors in individual or group counseling who assign the book as "homework" for clients between counseling sessions, or (5) trainers of employees in business and industry. Each of these uses is described below.

1. **Use of the ESDB System by an individual.** An individual could use this book as part of a self-help behavior modification program. Unit Two provides a structure for understanding behavior as well as the initial steps in changing behavior.

Each succeeding unit provides specific strategies for behavioral change, grouped according to their principal focus (thoughts, actions, or feelings). By completing each activity after reading the relevant text, an individual could make much progress toward behavioral change.

2. **Use of the ESDB System by participants in an ESDB Workshop.** Workshop leaders trained in group work will find this book extremely useful for the participants in an "Eliminating Self-Defeating Behaviors Workshop." Each unit can be the subject of one workshop meeting. The workshop can be composed of six meetings, each two to three hours in length, spread across a time span of up to six weeks. The activities have been designed so that some can be completed in workshop meetings while others can be done as homework. Workshop participants should be encouraged to "read ahead;" the more aware they are of the next meeting's topic, the more involved they will become in discussions and activities.

The following workshop schedule is recommended:

Week One: Cover Unit Two, including selected activities. Assign the remaining Unit Two activities and the text in Unit Three. Impress upon the participants the importance of using the tracking sheets (Activity 2.6) throughout the weeks of the workshop.

Week Two: Cover Unit Three, including selected activities. Assign the remaining Unit Three activities and the text in Unit Four. Encourage the participants to use a Thoughts Exits strategy during the week.

Week Three: Cover Unit Four, including selected activities. Assign the remaining Unit Four activities and the text in Unit Five. Encourage the participants to use an Actions Exit strategy during the week.

Week Four: Cover Unit Five, including selected activities. Assign the remaining Unit Five activities and the text in Unit Six. Encourage the participants to use a Feelings Exit strategy during the week.

Week Five: Cover Unit Six, including the activities. Have the participants examine their tracking sheets to determine if one strategy seemed to help more than the others they tried. Encourage them to begin thinking about the remaining work they need to do in order to develop more self-enhancing behaviors. If they are ready to plan their next steps, begin that work near the close of this meeting. Request that they continue thinking about the next steps they need to take during the week.

Week Six: Closing activities are necessary in this final meeting. Many workshop leaders ask participants to highlight the most significant experiences they had during the workshop. Help the participants complete their plans for future steps toward self-enhancing behaviors. If each participant is asked to describe his/her plans, the workshop often ends in a positive and motivating fashion.

These workshops are often conducted by college or university counseling centers, continuing education divisions, and mental health services.

3. **Use of the ESDB System by students in a class.** Many colleges and high schools offer classes which prepare students for academic success. This book could be used as a module that teaches students to overcome those behaviors which block them from reaching their academic goals.

   Other classes for which this book can be useful include Human Relations, The Helping Relationship, Techniques of Counseling, Group Procedures, and Consultation. Counseling psychology training programs and internships may be interested in this book since it is a ready-made psychoeducational program and can serve as a model for graduate students developing other psychoeducational programs.

4. **Use of the ESDB System by counselors in individual or group counseling.** Counselors and psychologists who work from a cognitive-behavioral framework could find the text useful in counseling and the activities useful as client homework. The "ESDB Circle" described in Unit Two and displayed throughout the book helps clients understand the interaction

that occurs between thoughts, actions, and feelings in the development of behaviors. The display at the end of Activity 3.5 demonstrates this interaction as well as the complexity of thoughts, consistent with the recent writings of Meichenbaum (1985).

The remaining parts of the book reinforce the notion of personal power and the benefits of systematic attempts at behavioral change. *By use of this book people focus their attention more on their thoughts, actions, and feelings, rather than on their prior difficulties in changing.* It subtly teaches that people need not "give up" if attempts to change are unsuccessful since so many methods for changing exist. People learn that a method *can* be found which will fit with their cognitive, affective, and behavioral styles. They simply need to keep trying.

5. **Use of the ESDB System by trainers of employees in business and industry.** Trainers of employees who conduct workshops to enhance supervisory skills or enable employees to eliminate behaviors that affect efficiency and productivity will find this system useful. For example, managers frequently "procrastinate" when it comes to performing unpleasant tasks or allow "the need to be perfect" to adversely affect the quality of their work life. Of course, many other applications exist for the ESDB System in the workplace.

For whatever purpose you use this book, you are apt to find it helpful if you desire to change your behavior. When the strategies in this book seem insufficient for accomplishing behavioral change, suggestions for other sources of help listed in Unit Six will guide you to appropriate health care providers.

You are now ready to proceed to Unit Two. You are to be commended for your willingness to take this "first step" toward changing your behavior. Many people would not have the courage or willingness to attempt behavioral change. To some extent this first step is the most important one, since people must admit that they have a problem before they can hope to find a solution to it. You have our best wishes as you take each additional step through the Eliminating Self-Defeating Behaviors System.

THE SDB CIRCLE

"What are Self-Defeating Behaviors and what can I do about them?"

The Eliminating Self-Defeating Behaviors (ESDB) System is designed to help you identify and eliminate behaviors that diminish the quality of your life.

The purposes of Unit Two are

1. to give you a basic knowledge of what self-defeating behaviors (SDBs) are,

2. to help you identify sources of energy that are causing you to maintain a pattern of self-defeating behaviors,

3. to help you identify sources of energy that can be drawn upon to eliminate self-defeating behaviors,

4. to enable you to describe a model that you can use to eliminate self-defeating behaviors,

5. to have you select one SDB for the purpose of practicing the ESDB System,

6. to help you track your self-defeating behaviors, and

7. to assist you in developing methods of reinforcing successful completion of each step in the ESDB System.

Defining Important Terms

Before we go any further, probably a helpful procedure would be to define the term "self-defeating behavior." While the definition of "eliminating" is generally well known, the definitions of "self-defeating" and "behavior" may not be as obvious. How would you define "self-defeating"? Take a minute to write your definition here.

_____

_____

_____

_____

Now consider "behavior." How would you define this term?

_____

_____

_____

_____

Behaviors, in their simplest form, are those things that we *do*. They are our actions and the aspects of our interactions with others that are observable. However, human behavior is very complex, and what we *do* is greatly affected by what we *think* and what we *feel*. Behavior in human beings actually has three components: *thoughts, actions,* and *feelings.* As you proceed through this book, we will make frequent reference to this concept and use it to help you understand better your own self-defeating behaviors. In addition, we will suggest ways for you to change your thoughts, actions, or feelings, which is the first step toward eliminating a self-defeating behavior.

Now let's consider the term "self-defeating." Any standard dictionary to define "defeating" uses such words as "to destroy or undo," "to deprive," "the prevention of success," or "to overcome or vanquish." All of these phrases suggest that something "bad" happens when one meets with defeat; that one does not accomplish a desired objective when one is "defeated." When you think of your own self-defeating behavior, you probably can think of how that behavior is keeping you from accomplishing something that is important to you.

The one word we haven't examined is "self." We all know what "self" means. It is you; it is who you are. Now let's put the two together: "self-defeating." Self-defeating behaviors, then, are limiting behaviors for which *you alone* are responsible. They limit you in your personal growth, in your relationships with others, in your career, and they can cause you to be physically unhealthy and emotionally unhappy. In general, they keep you from living a more complete life. To help you further understand the concept of "self-defeating behavior" please proceed to Activity 2.1, which deals with some examples of SDBs.

Activity 2.1

EXAMPLES OF SELF-DEFEATING BEHAVIORS

Goal

To better understand those behaviors that may be considered "self-defeating" by listing examples and comparing them with behaviors generally considered to be self-defeating by psychologists.

Directions

1. Review the list below of examples of SDBs suggested by people who have attend SDB courses and workshops.

   Examples of SDBs: Procrastination
   Striving for unrealistic goals
   Fear of failure
   Indecisiveness
   Trying to please "everyone"

2. List as many different examples of SDBs done by you and/or others as you can.

   _____

   _____

   _____

   _____

   _____

   _____

   Good! Your list may include some unique to you and/or some frequently listed by others.

3. When you are finished, compare your list with the following:

Examples of self-defeating behaviors:

Excessive excuse making	Reluctance to confront
Denying abilities	Compulsive actions
Acting guilty	Aggressiveness
Waking at irregular times	Avoiding challenges
Inability to accept compliments	Always apologizing
	Excessive guilt
Fear of rejection	Excessive eating
Excessive drinking	Inferiority
Excessive self-criticism	Self-doubt
Comparing self to others	Excessive passivity
Indecisiveness	Lack of assertiveness

4. Don't limit your concept of self-defeating behaviors to those on this list. Rather, use it to help you focus on your behaviors that could be considered "self-defeating."

Kathy's Response

2. List as many different examples of SDBs done by you and/or others as you can.

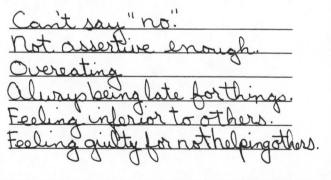

Can't say "no".
Not assertive enough.
Overeating
Always being late for things.
Feeling inferior to others.
Feeling guilty for not helping others.

Mike's Response

2. List as many different examples of SDBs done by you and/or others as you can.

Procrastination

I can't say "no"

Doubt myself

Always say the wrong thing

Feel guilty

The Energy Source and Prices Paid for SDBs

Self-defeating behaviors are learned, purposeful, and require energy to maintain. The purpose of SDBs is to protect you from having to respond to your world in a realistic and appropriate way. SDBs are enticing because they give you a reward for using them, such as temporary relief from tension and anxiety. This desire to avoid tension, anxiety, or other unpleasant feelings is the primary source of energy people use to maintain their self-defeating behavior patterns (Cudney, 1975).

Anxiety is a very powerful force and may cause you to perceive things differently than they really are. Anxiety may cause you to over- or under-react to threatening situations, and it may affect your ability to set goals and to move toward these goals. Because the use of SDBs can give you temporary relief from anxiety, the use of SDBs is extraordinarily habit forming, causing you to repeat them even though you know you are not behaving effectively.

Although avoidance of anxiety or other unpleasant feelings is a source of energy for maintaining SDBs, you also have a source of energy to draw upon to eliminate SDBs. This alternative source of energy is the recognition that you are paying a greater price in the long run for using your self-defeating behaviors (Cudney, 1975).

The prices you are paying can be placed into two distinct categories. In the first category are the actual prices you are paying, such as losing full control over your life, hurting others, feeling depressed, and experiencing impaired relationships. In the second category are the positive experiences you are missing, such as openness to growth, creativity, increased productivity at work, and the ability to be happy with yourself (Cudney, 1975).

You should now proceed to Activity 2.2 to learn more about the prices *you* are paying for behaving in self-defeating ways.

Activity 2.2

IDENTIFYING THE PRICES
YOU PAY FOR YOUR SDBs

Goals

1. To help you identify and clarify some of the prices you are paying for using self-defeating behaviors, and

2. to identify and clarify some of the experiences you are missing for engaging in your self-defeating behaviors.

Directions

1. Review the list of self-defeating behaviors in Activity 2.1.

2. In the spaces provided, list four self-defeating behaviors you use (remember, you may add to or omit ones you listed in Activity 2.1).

3. Try to identify the specific people who play a part in each SDB. List that person or these persons in part "a" under each SDB you list.

4. After each SDB, describe the general circumstances that are involved with your use of that SDB in "b."

5. In "c," write examples of negative prices you pay for participating in that SDB.

6. In "d," write examples of positive experiences missed because of that SDB.

7. Add additional sheets of paper, if needed, to add other SDBs that you want to examine.

Self-Defeating Behavior #1:_____

_____

    a. People who play a part in this SDB:_____

       _____

       _____

    b. Circumstances: _____

       _____

       _____

       _____

    c. Negative Prices I Pay:_____

       _____

       _____

       _____

    d. Positive Experiences I Miss:_____

       _____

       _____

       _____

Self-Defeating Behavior #2:_____

    a. People who play a part in this SDB:_____

       _____

       _____

       _____

b. Circumstances: _____

_____

_____

_____

c. Negative Prices I Pay:_____

_____

_____

_____

d. Positive Experiences I Miss:_____

_____

_____

_____

Self-Defeating Behavior #3:_____

a. People who play a part in this SDB:_____

_____

_____

_____

b. Circumstances: _____

_____

_____

_____

c. Negative Prices I Pay:_____

_____

_____

_____

d. Positive Experiences I Miss:_____

_____

_____

_____

Self-Defeating Behavior #4:_____

_____

a. People who play a part in this SDB:_____

_____

_____

b. Circumstances: _____

_____

_____

_____

c. Negative Prices I Pay:_____

_____

_____

_____

d. Positive Experiences I Miss:_____

_____

_____

_____

If you reflect on all the prices you pay and opportunities you miss because of your SDBs, you most likely will see many reasons to eliminate your dependence on SDBs.

The section that follows will help you identify just *one* SDB to use as you proceed through this book.

Kathy's Response

Self-Defeating Behavior #1: Not able to say "no" when other people ask me to help them.

a. People who play a part in this SDB: Just about everyone who asks for help.

b. Circumstances: Nothing specific — can happen in lots of different situations.

c. Negative Prices I Pay: Have less time for myself; do things I don't really want to do. Get mad at myself for not being able to say "no".

d. Positive Experiences I Miss: _Less time for the things I want to do. Not as happy as I think I could be._

Self-Defeating Behavior #2: _Feeling inferior._

a. People who play a part in this SDB: _Just about everyone I know._

b. Circumstances: _Whenever I'm doing something where I compare myself to others._

c. Negative Prices I Pay: _Not happy with myself. Other people put me down. I feel anxious a lot._

d. Positive Experiences I Miss: _I don't try new experiences. I'm shy around others. I'm not getting very far in my job. I don't meet the real neat guys._

Self-Defeating Behavior #3: _Lack of assertiveness._

    a. People who play a part in this SDB: _People who are authority figures-- like my boss, parents, or husband._

    b. Circumstances: _Situations where others want me to do something I don't agree with--but I don't let them know I disagree._

    c. Negative Prices I Pay: _Other people push me around. I get mad at myself for not speaking up._

    d. Positive Experiences I Miss: _Expressing my opinion. Feeling good about standing up to "Know-it-alls"._

Self-Defeating Behavior #4: _Excessive excuse-making._

a. People who play a part in this SDB: No one in particular.

b. Circumstances: Mostly when I fail or don't do well. Also when I don't live up to my own expectations.

c. Negative Prices I Pay: Feeling guilty-- other people seem to realize I'm making excuses.

d. Positive Experiences I Miss: I don't always try as hard as I could because I always seem to come up with excuses for my failures.

Mike's Response

Self-Defeating Behavior #1: I can't say "no."

a. People who play a part in this SDB: My sister and my girlfriend.

b. Circumstances: _When they ask me to do something I will do it even if I don't have the time._

c. Negative Prices I Pay: _I am rushed all the time_

d. Positive Experiences I Miss: _I can't belong to clubs because I don't have the time._

Self-Defeating Behavior #2: _Procrastination_

a. People who play a part in this SDB: _My boss and the people I work with._

b. Circumstances: _I would like to quit because I don't like the people I work with but its hard to go tell my boss._

c. Negative Prices I Pay: _I am unhappy._

d. Positive Experiences I Miss: _Being happy about going to work._

Self-Defeating Behavior #3: _Perfectionism_

    a. People who play a part in this SDB: _People I work with._

    b. Circumstances: _I want my work to be perfect but the people I work with accept sloppiness._

    c. Negative Prices I Pay: _I don't like my job -- therefore I'm unhappy._

    d. Positive Experiences I Miss: _Doing a job well and feeling good about myself._

Selecting Your Target SDB

As you proceed through this book you will find that learning the ESDB System will be easier if you concentrate on working on just one of your SDBs. Selecting the SDB which you will "target" for elimination takes some time and thought. To help you start, reexamine the list of SDBs which you just examined in Activity 2.2. Activity 2.3 will guide you as you choose a "target SDB," but before beginning, here are some tips you should consider.

1. Choose the SDB which you think will be the easiest for you to change. This way, you will be setting yourself up for success.

2. Choose the SDB which will be fun, yet challenging, to change. You need to help yourself make this learning process enjoyable, rather than unhappy, boring, or impossible.

3. Choose the SDB which seems "simpler" than the rest. You would make a mistake if you chose the SDB which you think is at the core of all the other SDBs you use. Once you learn how to eliminate SDBs by focusing your attempts on this simpler one, you will be able to tackle the one which is "at the root" of many others.

4. Choose an SDB which you know you are using now. Also, pick the SDB which happens often, not infrequently. The more chances you get to practice the ESDB System, the better is the probability that you will successfully learn to eliminate SDBs.

5. Choose an SDB which you know you can describe well. Remember that you must be able to identify the thoughts, actions, and feelings that comprise your SDB.

6. Finally, pick the SDB which you know you can observe yourself doing. You must be able to notice yourself using the SDB at the time it occurs, or very shortly afterwards.

Now proceed to Activity 2.3.

Activity 2.3

SELECTING YOUR TARGET SDB

Goal

    1. To select one SDB to eliminate and

    2. to learn methods to be used on other SDBs later.

Directions

    1. Examine the SDBs you listed in Activity 2.2. On the following lines, list those SDBs that you used frequently during the past few weeks.

    _____

    _____

    _____

    _____

    2. Now ask yourself, "Which of these SDBs listed in Item #1 can I *see* myself doing? Which of these might other people *see* me doing?"

    The following example is of a self-defeating behavior which cannot be observed. **Fear of Failure**—I can't see myself doing this; others can't see me doing this.

    The following example is of a self-defeating behavior of the type you are to list, one that can be observed. **Always apologizing**—I can see myself doing this; so can other people.

3. List in the space provided those SDBs in Item #1 which are "observable" self-defeating behaviors.

_____

_____

_____

4. Identify which of your "observable" SDBs listed in Item #3 that would be only moderately difficult to change. List those here.

_____

_____

5. From Item #4, choose the one SDB that you most want to change now. Write that here. This becomes your "target SDB."

_____

By selecting your target SDB, you have already completed a difficult, yet important, task. Now we want you to learn more about SDBs and how people use them. We will introduce you to the "SDB Circle," which is an important component of the ESDB System.

Kathy's Response

1. Examine the SDBs you listed in Activity 2.2. On the following lines, list those SDBs that you used frequently during the past few weeks.

Not being able to say "no" when people ask me to help them.

Feeling inferior.
Lack of assertiveness.

3. List in the space provided those SDBs in Item #1 which are "observable" self-defeating behaviors.

Not being able to say "no".
Not being assertive.

4. Identify which of your "observable" SDBs listed in Item #3 that would be only moderately difficult to change. List those here.

Not being able to say "no".

5. From Item #4, choose the one SDB that you most want to change now. Write that here. This becomes your "target SDB."

Not being able to say "no".

Mike's Response

1. Examine the SDBs you listed in Activity 2.2. On the following lines, list those SDBs that you used frequently during the past few weeks.

Procrastination
Perfectionism
Couldn't say "No"

3. List in the space provided those SDBs in Item #1 which are "observable" self-defeating behaviors.

Procrastination -- I can see myself doing this but others can't.

Perfectionism -- I see this -- others see this.
Can't say "No" -- I see myself
doing this -- others don't.

4. Identify which of your "observable" SDBs listed in Item #3 that would be only moderately difficult to change. List those here.

Can't say "No."
Procrastination

5. From Item #4, choose the one SDB that you most want to change now. Write that here. This becomes your "target SDB."

Procrastination

The Self-Defeating Behavior Circle

At the center of the Eliminating Self-Defeating Behaviors System is the SDB Circle. This circle can be used both to understand how people use self-defeating behaviors and how such behaviors can be overcome.

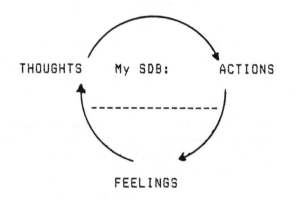

If you look at the circle, you will notice three points on it: *thoughts, actions,* and *feelings.* These three points represent the components of any behavior. Your behaviors are made up of certain thoughts, beliefs, and perceptions, followed by actions that you take, and by feelings or physical sensations. Those feelings are followed almost immediately by more thoughts, actions, and feelings. All of this happens so quickly that you rarely notice these three components of your behavior. Proceed to Activity 2.4 which is designed to help you pick out the thoughts, actions, and feelings which make up *your* SDB.

Activity 2.4

ANALYZING YOUR TARGET SDB

Goal

To identify those thoughts, actions, and feelings that comprise your target SDB.

Directions

1. Recall the last time you engaged in your target SDB. Remember things like (a) where you were, (b) whom you were with, (c) what you were doing, and (d) your mood at that time.

2. Examine the following example so that you will understand better how to use the SDB Circle.

   Example: The following is an example of a self-defeating behavior and the related thought, feeling, and action as recorded on the SDB Circle.

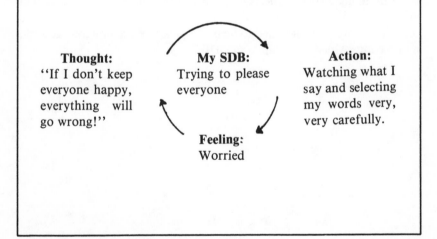

Thought:
"If I don't keep everyone happy, everything will go wrong!"

My SDB:
Trying to please everyone

Action:
Watching what I say and selecting my words very, very carefully.

Feeling:
Worried

3. Next, try to recall a thought you had as you began to use your SDB. Remember that a thought is just like a sentence that you repeat quietly to yourself. Write that thought on the circle below.

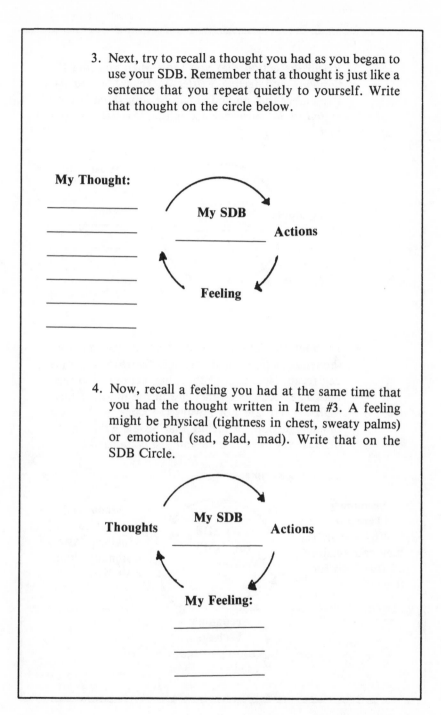

My Thought:

_____

_____

_____

_____

_____

My SDB

_____ **Actions**

Feeling

4. Now, recall a feeling you had at the same time that you had the thought written in Item #3. A feeling might be physical (tightness in chest, sweaty palms) or emotional (sad, glad, mad). Write that on the SDB Circle.

Thoughts   **My SDB**   **Actions**

_____

My Feeling:

_____

_____

_____

5. Recall the action that you took when you had the thoughts and feeling written in Items #3 and #4. Remember that an action can be something you *do* or *fail to do*. Write the action that was part of your SDB.

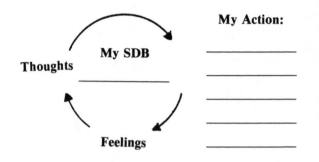

My Action:

_____

_____

_____

_____

_____

6. Examine the following SDB Circle of "secondary" thoughts, actions, and feelings. Sometimes people can recall "secondary" thoughts, actions, and feelings that occur when they are in the midst of their SDBs. These are not always the same as the first thought, action, or feeling that people write on the SDB circles like the ones you just completed.

Example:

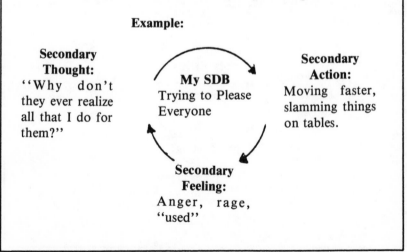

Secondary Thought:
"Why don't they ever realize all that I do for them?"

My SDB
Trying to Please Everyone

Secondary Action:
Moving faster, slamming things on tables.

Secondary Feeling:
Anger, rage, "used"

If you can recall any additional thoughts, actions, or feelings that occurred while you were in the midst of your SDB, write them on the circle that follows. (If you need more space than provided, write in the margin or on a separate sheet which you label as Activity 2.4 and keep for use in a later Activity.)

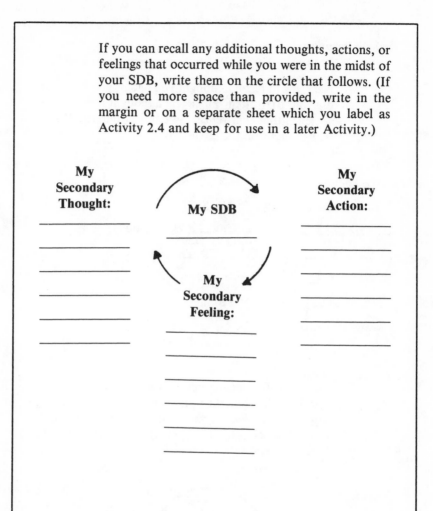

My Secondary Thought:

My SDB

My Secondary Action:

My Secondary Feeling:

These circles, on which you listed your first and secondary thoughts, actions, and feelings occurring during your SDB, show you the thoughts, actions, and feelings that comprise your self-defeating behavior.

The following section will explain more about the SDB Circle and how using it can help eliminate SDBs.

Kathy's Response

3. Next, try to recall a thought you had as you began to use your SDB. Remember that a thought is just like a sentence that you repeat quietly to yourself. Write that thought on the circle below.

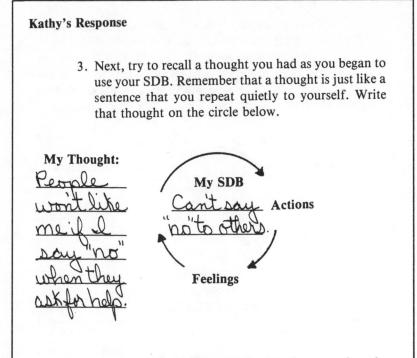

My Thought:

People won't like me if I say "no" when they ask for help.

My SDB

Can't say "no to others". Actions

Feelings

4. Now, recall a feeling you had at the same time that you had the thought written in Item #3. A feeling might be physical (tightness in chest, sweaty palms) or emotional (sad, glad, mad). Write that on the SDB Circle.

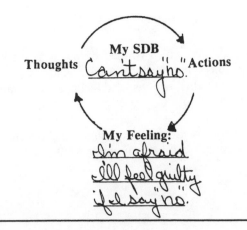

My SDB

Thoughts *Can't say "no".* Actions

My Feeling:

I'm afraid I'll feel guilty if I say "no".

5. Recall the action that you took when you had the thoughts and feeling written in Items #3 and #4. Remember that an action can be something you *do* or *fail to do*. Write the action that was part of your SDB.

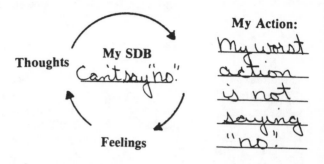

Thoughts

My SDB
Can't say "no".

Feelings

My Action:

My worst action is not saying "no".

6. Examine the following SDB Circle of "secondary" thoughts, actions, and feelings. Sometimes people can recall "secondary" thoughts, actions, and feelings that occur when they are in the midst of their SDBs. These are not always the same as the first thought, action, or feeling that people write on the SDB circles like the ones you just completed.

Example:

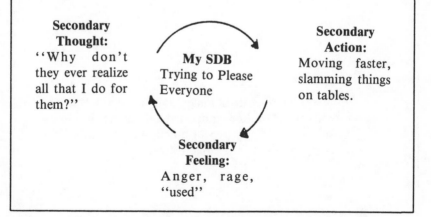

Secondary Thought:
"Why don't they ever realize all that I do for them?"

My SDB
Trying to Please Everyone

Secondary Action:
Moving faster, slamming things on tables.

Secondary Feeling:
Anger, rage, "used"

If you can recall any additional thoughts, actions, or feelings that occurred while you were in the midst of your SDB, write them on the circle that follows. (If you need more space than provided, write in the margin or on a separate sheet which you label as Activity 2.4 and keep for use in a later Activity.)

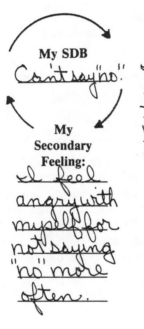

My Secondary Thought:
It's my duty to help others all the time.

My SDB
Can't say "no".

My Secondary Action:
I pretend I'm happy to help but I'm really not.

My Secondary Feeling:
I feel angry with myself for not saying "no" more often.

Mike's Response

3. Next, try to recall a thought you had as you began to use your SDB. Remember that a thought is just like a sentence that you repeat quietly to yourself. Write that thought on the circle below.

My Thought:

My boss is in a bad mood today. He will really chew me out. He'll never understand, so I'll wait until tomorrow to talk to him about the sloppy work done by other people working on the project.

My SDB

Actions

Feelings

4. Now, recall a feeling you had at the same time that you had the thought written in Item #3. A feeling might be physical (tightness in chest, sweaty palms) or emotional (sad, glad, mad). Write that on the SDB Circle.

Thoughts ⟶ **My SDB** ⟶ Actions

Procrastination

My Feeling:

*Butterflies
in my stomach
and I began
to sweat.
Anxious --
heart pounds.*

5. Recall the action that you took when you had the thoughts and feeling written in Items #3 and #4. Remember that an action can be something you *do* or *fail to do*. Write the action that was part of your SDB.

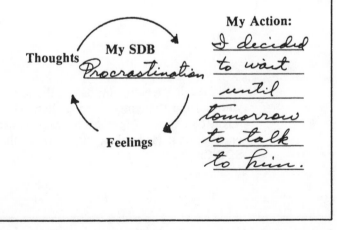

Thoughts ⟶ **My SDB**

Procrastination

My Action:

*I decided
to wait
until
tomorrow
to talk
to him.*

Feelings

6. Examine the following SDB Circle of "secondary" thoughts, actions, and feelings. Sometimes people can recall "secondary" thoughts, actions, and feelings that occur when they are in the midst of their SDBs. These are not always the same as the first thought, action, or feeling that people write on the SDB circles like the ones you just completed.

Example:

Secondary Thought

"Why don't they ever realize all that I do for them?"

My SDB

Trying to Please Everyone

Secondary Action:

Moving faster, slamming things on tables

Secondary Feeling:

Anger, rage, "used"

If you can recall any additional thoughts, actions, or feelings that occurred while you were in the midst of your SDB, write them on the circle that follows. (If you need more space than provided, write in the margin or on a separate sheet which you label as Activity 2.4 and keep for use in a later Activity.)

My Secondary Thought:

Why do I find it so hard to do anything I planned to do? I just can't do anything right!

My SDB

Procrastination

My Secondary Action:

Kept telling myself how stupid I am.

My Secondary Feeling:

Disappointment with myself. Feel bad, worthless.

More About the SDB Circle

In Activity 2.4, you learned that you can break your SDB down into three components: thoughts, actions, and feelings. You saw how these components build up on each other, trapping you in your SDBs. Negative or irrational thoughts sometimes lead to purposeless or frenzied actions. These actions may lead to feelings such as anxiety, fear, embarrassment, or anger, and these feelings, in turn, lead to more negative thoughts, actions, and feelings. The SDB Circle is a vicious one, taking you and your behavior 'round and 'round in a downward spiral of unhappiness.

Something which sounds as negative as this seems like something people would naturally avoid. Yet they don't. In fact, many people who engage in self-defeating behaviors report that they use their SDBs daily. Why is it that we go through the SDB Circle time and time again?

At least in part, the reason is because of *reinforcement*. Reinforcement is a dynamic process involving you and your environment. Your environment includes other people and perhaps certain events. Reinforcement "stamps-in" the self-defeating behavior (that is, the thoughts, actions, and feelings) which precede it. Consequently, the chances that you will again engage in the SDB always increase. In the following section you will learn more about reinforcement and its importance in understanding self-defeating behavior.

Reinforcement

In simple terms reinforcement is a reward that follows a specific behavior and causes that behavior to be repeated. You teach your dog to sit by rewarding (reinforcing) him/her when he/she learns to sit on your command. Similarly, you teach your children good manners by rewarding them when they act politely. When "rewards" follow behaviors and cause them to be repeated, psychologists refer to these rewards as "positive reinforcement." *Positive reinforcement* is a powerful force that affects much of your behavior, self-defeating and otherwise.

However, the concept of reinforcement is not that simple. In addition to positive reinforcement, another kind of reinforcement can have an equally powerful influence on your behavior. This other kind of reinforcement is called *negative reinforcement*. With negative reinforcement certain behaviors are repeated not because we anticipate getting a reward, but rather to avoid something unpleasant. For example, you don't speed when driving your car because you don't want a ticket, not because a policeman will stop you and compliment you for obeying the law! Similarly, a person may clean compulsively to avoid a roommate's (or spouse's) criticism or harrassment, not because praises or thanks are received. The avoidance of something unpleasant motivates us to repeat certain behaviors in negative reinforcement. The shaping of behavior through negative reinforcement can often be very subtle and unconscious, and in many instances we are behaving the way we do for the "wrong" reasons.

Often times our normal environment does not provide many opportunities for positive reinforcement. This probably accounts in part for why our self-defeating behaviors are learned in the first place. The use of positive reinforcement creates a much more positive and encouraging atmosphere than does the use of negative reinforcement and criticism. For example, for whom would your rather work: a boss who criticizes you every time you make a mistake, or one who compliments you when you do well? Under which boss do you think you would learn faster and perform better?

Now proceed to Activity 2.5 to see how reinforcement causes *you* to repeat your self-defeating behaviors.

Activity 2.5

HOW YOUR SDBs ARE REINFORCED

Goal

To learn how your SDBs are repeated due to positive and negative reinforcement.

Directions

In the spaces provided, list several SDBs that you listed in Activity 2.2. Be sure to include your target SDB as the first one listed. Using these same SDBs, think about examples of positive and negative reinforcement that may cause you to repeat these behaviors. Keep in mind that you repeat your SDBs for a reason(s). These "reasons" can often be described in terms of "reinforcement," that is, either "rewards" or behaviors that help you avoid unpleasant consequences.

Example:

SDB: Excessive cleaning.

Positive Reinforcers (Rewards): Compliments from friends or family members. Feeling good about myself.

Negative Reinforcers (Avoidance of Unpleasantness): Afraid husband will yell at or criticize me. Am afraid people will think I'm sloppy. Will feel I'm not a good housekeeper.

Note: In this example, cleaning house to receive the positive reinforcers described above is not necessarily self-defeating. However, *excessive* cleaning to avoid the negative reinforcers described above may very well be self-defeating. In this case the person is behaving in an excessive manner, doing something that is not fun and in fact unpleasant, and all for the *wrong* reasons!

Now, you try to analyze several of your SDBs in terms of positive and negative reinforcement.

SDB #1 (Your target SDB):_____

    Positive Reinforcers:_____

    _____

    Negative Reinforcers:_____

_____

SDB #2:_____

    Positive Reinforcers:_____

    _____

    Negative Reinforcers:_____

    _____

SDB #3:_____

    Positive Reinforcers:_____

    _____

    Negative Reinforcers:_____

    _____

Very good! By now you should have a better understanding of why you behave the way you do when it comes to self-defeating behavior. This is another important step in eliminating these unwanted behaviors.

Kathy's Response

SDB #1 (Your target SDB): Not being able to say no.
Positive Reinforcers: People seem to like me more. I feel good when I help others.
Negative Reinforcers: I avoid feeling guilty when I help people.

SDB #2: Feeling inferior.
Positive Reinforcers: I can't think of anything positive about feeling inferior.
Negative Reinforcers: By feeling inferior, I tend to avoid trying new or different things which helps me avoid situations where I might fail.

SDB #3: Excessive excuse-making.
Positive Reinforcers: My excuses make me feel better about my failures temporarily.
Negative Reinforcers: I avoid feeling like it was my fault.

Mike's Response

SDB #1 (Your target SDB): *Procrastination*
 Positive Reinforcers: *My boss tells me I do a good job and that I can get along better than anyone he knows.*

 Negative Reinforcers: *I feel bad about my work -- its not as good as it could be because the others are sloppy.*

SDB #2: *Perfectionism*
 Positive Reinforcers: *People compliment me which makes me feel good.*

 Negative Reinforcers: *Anxious feelings -- I can never get it right.*

SDB #3: *Can't say "No."*
 Positive Reinforcers: *People tell me how nice I am.*

 Negative Reinforcers: *I can't get my own job done.*

Tracking Your Target SDB

The first step in changing a behavior is understanding that behavior thoroughly. This holds true for self-defeating behaviors as well. You must find out when and how often your SDB occurs. You cannot rely on your hunches or recollections. You need to become a "scientist" if you are to eliminate your SDB, and tracking it is part of the scientific process you must use. Activity 2.6 will help you learn how to track your own use of your target SDB. Extra worksheets for this exercise are included since you will be tracking your SDB on a weekly basis.

Activity 2.6

TRACKING YOUR SDBs

Goal

To understand your current behavior so that you may design a strategy to eliminate those behaviors that are self-defeating.

Directions

1. Review the sample tracking sheet on the following page.

2. Put today's date in the box labled "Day 1." Then, whenever you notice your SDB, put a mark (/) in the appropriate box. For example, if your SDB occurs once this afternoon, you will put a mark (/) in the box labled "PM" under "Day 1." If it occurs five times tomorrow evening, you will put a mark after each occurrence (/////) in the box labeled "After 5 PM" under "Day 2."

3. At the bottom of the tracking sheet, periodically write what you were doing when your SDB occurred. This will help you later in understanding what, if anything, is associated with your SDB.

4. Use the tracking sheets that follow the sample. Enough are provided for 7 weeks. Write the correct date under "Day 1" and write the week number on each sheet.

   Note: An important procedure is to use the sheets daily and to note each time that you engage in a self-defeating behavior. The first step in changing a behavior is understanding it thoroughly. You must find out when and how often your SDBs occur. You cannot rely on your hunches or your recollections. You need to become more scientific if you are to learn to eliminate your SDBs, and tracking them is part of the scientific process.

Sample SDB Tracking Sheet

Week of May 11

	Day 1	Day 2	Day 3	Day 4	Day 5	Day 6	Day 7
AM							
PM	/						
After 5 PM		//// /					

Notes:

SDB: Excessive fear

Where?   Usually at home

With whom? I was alone

Thoughts?   "I'll never be relaxed in this place!"

Actions?   I paced back and forth a lot.

Feelings?   Scared, lonely, empty feeling in my stomach.

SDB Tracking Sheet

Week of_____

	Day 1	Day 2	Day 3	Day 4	Day 5	Day 6	Day 7
AM							
PM							
After 5 PM							

Notes:

   SDB:

   Where?

   With whom?

   Thoughts?

   Actions?

   Feelings?

SDB Tracking Sheet

Week   of_____

	Day 1	Day 2	Day 3	Day 4	Day 5	Day 6	Day 7
AM							
PM							
After 5 PM							

Notes:

   SDB:

   Where?

   With whom?

   Thoughts?

   Actions?

   Feelings?

SDB Tracking Sheet

Week of_____

	Day 1	Day 2	Day 3	Day 4	Day 5	Day 6	Day 7
AM							
PM							
After 5 PM							

Notes:

    SDB:

    Where?

    With whom?

    Thoughts?

    Actions?

    Feelings?

SDB Tracking Sheet

Week of_____

	Day 1	Day 2	Day 3	Day 4	Day 5	Day 6	Day 7
AM							
PM							
After 5 PM							

Notes:

    SDB:

    Where?

    With whom?

    Thoughts?

    Actions?

    Feelings?

SDB Tracking Sheet

Week   of_____

	Day 1	Day 2	Day 3	Day 4	Day 5	Day 6	Day 7
AM							
PM							
After 5 PM							

Notes:

    SDB:

    Where?

    With whom?

    Thoughts?

    Actions?

    Feelings?

SDB Tracking Sheet

Week of_____

	Day 1	Day 2	Day 3	Day 4	Day 5	Day 6	Day 7
AM							
PM							
After 5 PM							

Notes:

    SDB:

    Where?

    With whom?

    Thoughts?

    Actions?

    Feelings?

SDB Tracking Sheet

Week of_____

	Day 1	Day 2	Day 3	Day 4	Day 5	Day 6	Day 7
AM							
PM							
After 5 PM							

Notes:

    SDB:

    Where?

    With whom?

    Thoughts?

    Actions?

    Feelings?

Kathy's Response

SDB Tracking Sheet

Week of _April 7_

	Day 1	Day 2	Day 3	Day 4	Day 5	Day 6	Day 7
AM	//	/	///	/	/	//	/
PM	/	/	/	/	/	//	//
After 5 PM	/	//		//	/		///

Notes:

SDB: Can't say "no" when people ask for help.

Where? Mostly at work, but also at home.

With whom? Co-workers and friends.

Thoughts? Why do I get into these situations? Why do I worry so much about what others think?

Actions? I say "yes" when I really don't want to.

Feelings? Guilt mostly; frustrated and angry with myself.

Mike's Response

SDB Tracking Sheet

Week of _____ April 7 _____

	Day 1	Day 2	Day 3	Day 4	Day 5	Day 6	Day 7
AM	///	////	////	//	///	////	///
PM	/		/				/
After 5 PM							

Notes:

SDB: *Procrastination*

Where? *At work*

With whom? *Joe*

Thoughts? *If I tell Joe that I don't like doing his work, we will have an argument.*

Actions? *I didn't tell him.*

Feelings? *Angry with myself.*

Exiting From the SDB Circle

If SDBs are made up of the three components previously described, then, as you can deduce, you can eliminate SDBs by "breaking out" of the SDB Circle at one of the three points on it, just like short-circuiting an electrial circuit. When you create a short circuit, a light on that circuit will no longer operate. Similarly, if you *exit* from the SDB Circle by changing your thoughts *or* your actions *or* your feelings, you will have "short-circuited" the SDB. Then, if you are reinforced for *exiting,* you begin to "stamp in" a new behavior: a self-enhancing behavior. No longer will you be defeating yourself. Instead, you will actually be helping yourself!

In the units to come you will have the opportunity to learn more about "exiting" the SDB Circle and you will complete some helpful activities.

Conclusion

Congratulations! In having learned how to identify, analyze, and track your SDB, you have accomplished an important first step in learning how to eliminate self-defeating behaviors. You have learned, too, the prices you pay and the reasons you continue to use SDBs. In the units that follow, you will develop a greater understanding of the nature of self-defeating behaviors. You also will acquire the skills necessary to cope more effectively with your own SDBs. You will find that you may draw upon these skills whenever necessary. They should serve you well throughout the rest of your life.

You will now take the next step in the strategy for eliminating self-defeating behaviors.

THE THOUGHTS EXIT

**"How can I change the way
I think about my SDBs?"**

So far you have learned what self-defeating behaviors are. In this unit you will learn that a relationship often exists between "irrational beliefs" and self-defeating behaviors. You also will learn how you can eliminate your SDBs by changing your irrational beliefs as well as by changing the way you think about yourself and your environment.

The purposes of Unit Three are

1. to help you understand better the thoughts associated with your SDBs;

2. to help you distinguish between the thoughts and feelings associated with your SDBs;

3. to teach you to exit the SDB Circle by changing your irrational beliefs to rational, productive beliefs; and

4. to enable you to employ the "Metathoughts Method" as a second way of exiting the SDB Circle at the thoughts exit.

Review of Unit Two

In Unit Two you were introduced to the Self-Defeating Behavior Circle and to the use of tracking sheets for collecting data about your target SDB. Let's review each of these.

The Self-Defeating Behavior Circle explains how self-defeating behaviors evolve and how you can attempt to eliminate them.

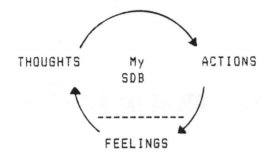

THOUGHTS   My   ACTIONS
              SDB

FEELINGS

You will recall that SDBs are composed of thoughts, actions, and feelings which build upon each other, are reinforced, and become "stamped in."

You learned that once you "exit" from the Self-Defeating Behavior Circle by changing either a thought, action, or feeling, you will have taken the first step toward eliminating your SDB. You also learned to follow-up that step with positive thoughts, actions, and feelings to help stamp-in new self-enhancing behavior patterns. Consequently, the chances that you will engage in the SDB again will decrease and eventually you will have eliminated the SDB altogether.

The purpose of the tracking sheet is to help you more thoroughly understand your SDB. This means that you must know when and how often the SDB occurs and what it is that you are doing when the SDB occurs. Also, the tracking sheets will help you learn which strategy for exiting the SDB Circle works best for you. The tracking sheets provide you with feedback about your attempts to eliminate your self-defeating behavior.

Remember the following points:

1. SDBs are learned behaviors.

2. SDBs can be "short-circuited" by exiting at either the thoughts, actions, or feelings exits on the circle.

3. Once you exit using a strategy which you will learn in this book, then you must be sure that you

    a. follow-up the strategy with positive thoughts, actions, and feelings;

    b. reward yourself for doing all of this; and

    c. continue tracking your SDBs.

If you find that you are having difficulty recalling the material from Unit Two, take time now to review and reread it. Pay special attention to Activity 2.4, where you will find the SDB Circle on which you wrote the thoughts, actions, and feelings you have when you engage in your SDB.

Differences Between Thoughts and Feelings

In order to exit the SDB Circle at the thoughts exit, you must be able to accurately determine the thoughts associated with your SDB. Although this might seem to be a fairly simple task, for many people it isn't. Not uncommonly people who are analyzing their SDB become confused as to which are feelings and which are thoughts; that is, to label something as a feeling when it is really a thought. For example, someone might say, "I feel like other people don't like me." Although the person might believe this is a feeling, it is not! It is a thought or belief that the person holds.

To help you in eliminating SDBs you must understand that "feelings" are emotions. They include such emotions as anger, guilt, depression, sadness, and anxiety. Associated with your feelings (emotions) are physical reactions such as increased heart rate, sweating, "butterflies in the stomach," or in some instances a depression of bodily functions. Feelings (emotions) are an important part of your SDBs, but they are very different from your thoughts. To properly analyze your SDB you must be able to distinguish between thoughts and feelings.

Now proceed to Activity 3.1 which will help you distinguish between thoughts and feelings.

Activity 3.1

DISTINGUISHING BETWEEN THOUGHTS AND FEELINGS

Goal

To learn to discriminate between thoughts and feelings.

Directions

1. Read the following statements and in the space provided write a "T" if you think the statement is a thought or an "F" if you think the statement is a feeling.

   Example:

   T "I feel like other people don't like me."

   This statement may seem like a feeling, particularly since it includes the phrase, "I feel." However, it is really a thought or belief held by this person, probably caused by shyness and feelings of inferiority.

   Now you try...

   a. _____ "I feel like I can't do anything right."

   b. _____ "I am angry and feel like hitting someone!"

c. _____ "I can't seem to make up my mind or make important decisions."

d. _____ "I feel so sad and depressed I could just sit down and cry."

e. _____ "I am shy and have trouble making new friends."

f. _____ "I hurt anyone who gets close to me."

g. _____ "I feel bad that I hurt his feelings."

2. Check your answers with those shown on the next page.

Answers to Activity 3.1

a. **T**—This is a belief that this person holds about himself/herself probably based on perceptions of past failures and an exaggeration of the importance of these failures.

b. **F**—This is an expression of a feeling, in this case a strong feeling of anger and aggression.

c. **T**—This is a belief or thought based on a "perception of self." No specific emotion is being expressed here.

d. **F**—This is clearly an expression of an emotional response, in this case sadness and depression.

e. **T**—This is another sample of a thought, although some emotions that may be associated with it are guilt or inferiority.

f. **T**—No particular emotion is being expressed here. This person simply believes that he/she hurts people who get "too close."

g. **F**—This statement is an expression of a feeling of sadness over having hurt someone's feelings.

Kathy's Response

> **Now you try...**

> a. __F__ "I feel like I can't do anything right."

> b. __F__ "I am angry and feel like hitting someone!"

> c. __T__ "I can't seem to make up my mind or make important decisions."

> d. __F__ "I feel so sad and depressed I could just sit down and cry."

> e. __T__ "I am shy and have trouble making new friends."

> f. __T__ "I hurt anyone who gets close to me."

> g. __F__ "I feel bad that I hurt his feelings."

Mike's Response

> **Now you try...**

> a. __T__ "I feel like I can't do anything right."

> b. __F__ "I am angry and feel like hitting someone!"

> c. __T__ "I can't seem to make up my mind or make important decisions."

d. _F_ "I feel so sad and depressed I could just sit down and cry."

e. _T_ "I am shy and have trouble making new friends."

f. _T_ "I hurt anyone who gets close to me."

g. _F_ "I feel bad that I hurt his feelings."

Changing Your Thoughts and Beliefs

One strategy for exiting from the SDB Circle is based on a concept developed by Dr. Albert Ellis (1977). Ellis' model, which he called the "ABCs of Rational Living," explains how people can change their thoughts and beliefs about themselves. Ellis (Ellis & Grieger, 1977) claimed that irrational beliefs are at the bottom of most problems. If you change your irrational beliefs (thoughts) to rational, more productive beliefs, you will experience many positive effects. One of those positive effects can be the elimination of self-defeating behaviors.

The following diagram illustrates Ellis' model.

```
A  ------------>  i B  ------------>  i C  ------------>  -E
Activating        irrational      !   irrational         negative
Event             Beliefs         !   Consequences       Effects
   \                              D
    \                             Dispute
     \                            !
      \                          \ ! /
       \------->  r B  ------------>  r C  ------------>  +E
                  rational            rational           positive
                  Beliefs             Consequences       Effects
```

According to Ellis, your beliefs about events lead to certain consequences and effects. This is a powerful statement. It suggests that what you *think* about yourself and the world around you causes you to act in certain ways and have certain feelings, which in turn stimulates additional thoughts.

Unfortunately, people rarely recognize that the causes of their feelings and actions come from themselves. At one time or another, you have probably said, "He made me do it!" or "It's because of YOU that I feel so sad!" Now you are learning that this is an incorrect statement. No one makes you do anything; you do something because of what *you* think about another person's words or actions. Likewise, no one makes you feel sad; you feel sad because of what *you think* about another person, situation, or experience.

The diagram of Ellis' model illustrates this. An activating event (A) is an event or action which disturbs you. The belief (B) is the thought which you have about the event, and it can be rational or irrational. A rational belief is one which can be supported by evidence. It is an accurate thought about what is truly happening. An irrational belief, on the other hand, is difficult, if not impossible, to support with evidence. It is neither accurate nor realistic, and it is often an exaggeration. A belief implies that you are predicting what will happen next (Cronkhite, 1976). The consequences (C) include your resulting feelings and actions. The effects (E) are what happens to you because of all of this; for example, whether you are relaxed or anxious, in-control or out-of-control.

By looking at the diagram, you will see that irrational beliefs lead to irrational consequences and negative effects. Rational beliefs, however, lead to rational consequences and positive effects. The more often you experience positive effects, the more often you will think in rational ways. If you will recall the information in Unit Two on reinforcement, you will notice that this last statement sounds a lot like positive reinforcement. In fact, it is. Positive effects are very reinforcing, and they result in your repeating whatever it was which preceded them. In this case, rational beliefs preceded the positive effects.

Ellis and Harper (1975) pointed out that disputing (D) irrational beliefs (iB) will decrease negative effects (-E). Irrational beliefs are disputed by challenging and questioning them. Each time you successfully dispute your irrational beliefs, you revert to the use of rational, more productive beliefs. That sends you to the positive level of the diagram. The chances of developing rational, productive beliefs increase.

One clue that your thoughts are irrational is the presence of "shoulds, oughts, or musts" (Ellis & Harper, 1975). Doing things that *other people* think you "should do" or "ought to do" may not be good for *you*. The views of others should not dominate your thinking or lead you to beliefs about yourself that are not accurate. You will need to always test your beliefs and thoughts for accuracy. Similarly, doing things that *you* think you "should" do may not always be good for you.

Now proceed to Activity 3.2 which will help you learn to dispute the validity of thoughts and beliefs.

Activity 3.2

DISPUTING AND FINDING ALTERNATIVES TO IRRATIONAL BELIEFS

Goals

1. To examine the irrational beliefs listed below,

2. to attempt to dispute them, and

3. to write alternative beliefs that are more rational and productive.

Directions

Analyze the following irrational beliefs by completing "a" and "b" for each belief listed below.

Example:

Irrational belief: "I can't do anything right!"

    a. Why it might be irrational: It is unlikely that someone can't do "anything" right. This person is probably exaggerating in this instance because of feelings of inferiority.

    b. Alternative, more productive belief: "I can't do some things as well as I'd like to, but no one's perfect. My failures shouldn't stop me from trying new experiences."

Now analyze the following irrational beliefs:

1. Irrational belief: "No one will ever like me if I say 'no' when they ask for help!"

    a. Why it might be irrational:_____

       _____

       _____

       _____

    b. Alternative, more productive belief:_____

       _____

       _____

       _____

2. Irrational belief: "How awful it will be if I can't get this job!"

    a. Why it might be irrational:_____

       _____

       _____

       _____

    b. Alternative, more productive belief:_____

       _____

       _____

       _____

3. Irrational belief: "If he/she leaves me, I'll never find another person to be with!"

    a. Why it might be irrational:_____

       _____

       _____

       _____

    b. Alternative, more productive belief:_____

       _____

       _____

       _____

4. Irrational belief: "How awful it will be if I cannot pass this test!"

    a. Why it might be irrational:_____

       _____

       _____

       _____

    b. Alternative, more productive belief:_____

       _____

       _____

       _____

After you complete your practice in analyzing examples of irrational beliefs and after reviewing Kathy's and Mike's responses, proceed to Activity 3.3 which will help you dispute more of your irrational beliefs associated with and find more productive alternatives for your target SDB.

Kathy's Response

Now analyze the following irrational beliefs:

1. Irrational belief: "No one will ever like me if I say 'no' when they ask for help!"

    a. Why it might be irrational: _I guess it's unlikely that "no one" will like me if I say "no" at least sometimes._

    b. Alternative, more productive belief: _Maybe I shouldn't worry so much about what other people think. It's OK to say "no" at least some of the time and put myself first once in a while._

2. Irrational belief: "How awful it will be if I can't get this job!"

    a. Why it might be irrational: There are other jobs, and losing out on one probably isn't that awful.

    b. Alternative, more productive belief: I'll be disappointed if I don't get this job, but I won't let that stop me from trying again.

3. Irrational belief: "If he/she leaves me, I'll never find another person to be with!"

    a. Why it might be irrational: I guess there really are other people who I could like and who would like me. (There are plenty of fish in the sea!).

    b. Alternative, more productive belief: I'll try to meet new people if he leaves me because I think I'm a good person.

4. Irrational belief: "How awful it will be if I cannot pass this test!"

   a. Why it might be irrational: _It's only one test, it can't be that important._

   b. Alternative, more productive belief: _If I fail this test, I'll just have to try harder on the next one._

Mike's Response

Now analyze the following irrational beliefs:

1. Irrational belief: "No one will ever like me if I say 'no' when they ask for help!"

   a. Why it might be irrational: _Because someone might not mind -- everyone is not alike._

   b. Alternative, more productive belief: _Some people might not like me for saying "no" but not everyone._

2. Irrational belief: "How awful it will be if I can't get this job!"

    a. Why it might be irrational: _Because others might not see it as so bad, and I can go on to another job, anyway!_

    b. Alternative, more productive belief: _I might be disappointed if I don't get it, but I can try again tomorrow._

3. Irrational belief: "If he/she leaves me, I'll never find another person to be with!"

    a. Why it might be irrational: _There are so many people that it's impossible that there is "no one."_

    b. Alternative, more productive belief: _There are people who would find me attractive._

4. Irrational belief: "How awful it will be if I cannot pass this test!"

    a. Why it might be irrational: *My life won't end if I don't pass this test.*

    b. Alternative, more productive belief: *This test is important, but not as important as my life.*

Activity 3.3

YOUR TARGET SDB AND
ITS IRRATIONAL BELIEFS

Goals

1. To examine the irrational beliefs associated with your target SDB, and

2. to develop productive alternative thoughts.

Directions

1. Refer back to Unit Two, Activity 2.4, where you listed the thoughts associated with your target SDB. In order to complete this activity, designate the first thought you listed "thought a" and the second thought "thought b." If you listed additional thoughts, designate them "thought c" and "thought d."

2. Using the same procedure as in Activity 3.2, list each thought or belief below and try to find reasons why each one may be irrational. Then try to write a more productive, rational, alternative belief.

Thought   a:_____

_____

Why "thought a" might be irrational:_____

_____

_____

_____

Alternative, more productive thought:_____

_____

_____

_____

Thought   b:_____

_____

Why "thought b" might be irrational:_____

_____

_____

_____

Alternative, more productive thought:_____

_____

_____

_____

Thought   c:_____

_____

Why "thought c" might be irrational:_____

_____

_____

Alternative, more productive thought:_____

_____

_____

_____

Thought   d:_____

_____

Why "thought d" might be irrational:_____

_____

_____

_____

_____

Alternative, more productive thought:_____

_____

_____

_____

Very good! You now have learned one strategy for eliminating SDBs at the thoughts exit. After reviewing Kathy's and Mike's responses, proceed to the next section where you will learn another strategy called the "metathoughts method" as well as two ways in which you can employ that strategy.

Kathy's Response

2. Using the same procedure as in Activity 3.2, list each thought or belief below and try to find reasons why each one may be irrational. Then try to write a more productive, rational, alternative belief.

Thought a: *People won't like me if I say "no" when they ask for help.*

Why "thought a" might be irrational: *I guess I don't know that for sure, and maybe I shouldn't expect to be "liked by "everyone".*

Alternative, more productive thought: *If some people don't like me for not helping them, then maybe I'll just have to learn to accept that.*

Thought b: *It's my duty to help others all the time.*

Why "thought b" might be irrational: I guess it doesn't make sense to never think about myself. I guess I go to far in helping others.

Alternative, more productive thought: It's OK to think about myself and put my needs first -- at least some of the time.

Thought c: I feel good about myself when I help others.

Why "thought c" might be irrational: I don't think there is anything irrational about this belief.

Alternative, more productive thought: OK as is.

Thought d: I must be the only one who can help these people -- why else would they ask me?

Why "thought d" might be irrational: _It's probably not very realistic to believe I'm the only one who can help others. They probably ask me a lot because I always say "yes"._

Alternative, more productive thought: _It's OK to say "no" sometimes and lot people find someone else to help them._

Mike's Response

2. Using the same procedure as in Activity 3.2, list each thought or belief below and try to find reasons why each one may be irrational. Then try to write a more productive, rational, alternative belief.

Thought a: _My boss is in a bad mood today and will really chew me out._

Why "thought a" might be irrational: _I may be only imagining how he feels_ and if he is upset, I need to know what he sees as the problem.

Alternative, more productive thought: My boss may be upset, and if he is, I could explore with him what problems he sees. This could only help me.

Thought b: Why is it so hard to do anything I planned to do?

Why "thought b" might be irrational: Only somethings are difficult. Actually I do a lot of things well.

Alternative, more productive thought: Some things are difficult to do even when plans are made. If I accept that, I won't get down on myself so much.

Thought c: I can't do anything right.

Why "thought c" might be irrational: _Certainly_
I can do some things right.
Actually I do pretty well on
my job and at home.

Alternative, more productive thought: _Some_
things I don't do well, but
most things I do very well --
after all, I don't have
to be perfect.

Changing the Way You Think

The second strategy for exiting at the Thoughts Exit is based upon Donald Meichenbaum's Cognitive-Behavior Modification (1977) and a technique he developed, called "Stress Inoculation Training" (1985). This strategy is called the "Metathoughts Method" because it requires that you "think about your thinking." The goal of the metathoughts method is to have you develop a new way of thinking as you attempt a task.

You can use the Metathoughts Method in two ways. First, you can examine things you say to yourself as you are trying to perform a task. If your "self-talk" appears to block you from a successful performance, then you can change the way you talk to yourself in order to help yourself perform better. Second, you can examine your basic beliefs about your environment and your opportunities within it. If your basic beliefs are causing you to behave in ways that hurt you, you can attempt to find new ways of looking at your environment and opportunities. As you do this, you will change your thoughts, actions, and feelings, and the chances are great that you will be far more successful when you attempt tasks.

Let's examine these two ways of using the metathoughts method more closely.

1. **Talking to yourself more productively.** Sometimes the very things people say to themselves cause them trouble! Imagine trying to do a complicated crossword puzzle. Throughout your attempt, you mumble to yourself, "My vocabulary is terrible; I don't have any business trying to do a crossword puzzle as difficult as this." What do you think the chances would be for you to successfully complete that puzzle?

Donald Meichenbaum (1977) recommended that people learn to talk to themselves in ways that are relevant and helpful toward completing a task. In the example above, you would be distracting yourself with thoughts that are not helpful at all if you said those things to yourself. If, on the other hand, you talked to yourself in ways that would keep you calm and guide you through the task, your words could be very helpful. For example, you might say to yourself, "That was a difficult clue; while I don't know that word, there are lots of other clues here. Slow down, take a deep breath, and try to get the next word on the puzzle."

Of course, the tasks that you face each day are more complicated than crossword puzzles. Sometimes you try to resolve problems with other people, while at other times you might be attempting a job that requires a great deal of precision. No matter what the task is that you are facing, if you talk to yourself in positive ways that guide you through the task, you will increase your ability to do your best at that job.

Some people have found that, by asking themselves the following questions, they are able to successfully guide themselves through their tasks. In fact, some people put these questions on a card that they carry with them for use when they need it. The questions are as follows:

- What is my problem?
- What is my plan to solve my problem?
- Have I enacted my plan?
- Did my plan help?

When you use these questions, you keep your thoughts focused on solving your problem. If your plan doesn't help, then simply develop a better plan. That is far superior to chastising yourself for failing—and it will get you to a solution far sooner!

Before considering the second way of using the Metathoughts Method, try practicing this first way. In the next activity, you will have an opportunity to consider your SDB and how you can talk differently to yourself to break out of the SDB Circle. You will create a card that will help you focus your attention on solving your problem, thus making your SDB solution your prime objective when you catch yourself engaging in your SDB.

Activity 3.4

TALKING TO YOURSELF
TO ELIMINATE YOUR SDB

Goal

To help you develop words you can say to yourself which will guide you out of your self-defeating behavior.

Directions

1. Think about your self-defeating behavior.

2. Recall where it occurs and what you are doing. If you were to talk to yourself so that you would guide yourself out of that SDB, what would you need to say?

3. Try to identify how to calm yourself, keep your attention focused on your task, and give yourself directions for what to do next.

   As an example, a person with "test anxiety" as a self-defeating behavior might say the following: "OK. I didn't know the answer to that question, but that was only one question. There are plenty of others that I can answer. Slow down, and take a deep breath. There, that's better. Now go on to the next question and answer that one."

4. Write here what you could say to yourself that would help you break-out of your SDB.

   _____

   _____

_____

_____

_____

5. Read what you just wrote. Will those words keep you
   attending to the thing you are trying to do, rather
   than keep you caught in the middle of your SDB? If
   those words will guide you out of your SDB, then
   you have created one Metathoughts Method that
   could work for you.

6. Write these words from Step 4 on a card that you can
   carry with you and use whenever you need it. You
   might simply want to use the questions that were
   listed on the preceding page. If you do, write those
   on a card instead.

Kathy's Response

4. Write here what you could say to yourself that would
   help you break-out of your SDB.

   Do people always need just me?
   What did I really want to do?
   It's OK to put myself first
   sometimes. I need to be se-
   cure enough with myself to
   say "no" sometimes.

Mike's Response

4. Write here what you could say to yourself that would help you break-out of your SDB.

I know what I want to say to my boss. If it's difficult, I can rehearse before talking with him. Talk to him when he is not overextended.

2. **Altering your basic beliefs.** The second Metathoughts Method involves altering your basic beliefs. These basic beliefs that you hold about your environment or your opportunities within the environment have strong effects on your thoughts, actions, and feelings. A few examples might help you understand this.

People often fear something that has, in reality, a very small probability of occurring. Their fear is probably rooted in a belief that they are helpless in a particular situation, or sometimes, helpless in *all* situations.

When people hold a basic belief that they are helpless, they look for information that will confirm their helplessness in any situation in which they find themselves (Frank, 1974; Meichenbaum, 1985). When trying to resolve a dispute at work, such a person will view another's hostility as evidence that "I'll never get anywhere with this person! I might as well give up!" Notice how helplessness is often tied with hopelessness.

The automatic thoughts that people say to themselves as they are gathering evidence to confirm their basic beliefs affect their actions and feelings. Those persons who repeat the preceding statement would act with resignation and feel depressed. They become caught in the self-defeating behavior circle.

Interestingly, people often fail to realize that they could use other basic beliefs about their environment or opportunities. These other beliefs could be much more realistic. For example, suppose a girl was having difficulty with her boyfriend and things did not go her way. As a result she could develop the belief that "it's hopeless." Yet, if she has faced situations in which things did not go her way many times, she also must be a person with a great deal of "stick-to-it-iveness."

If her belief, "it's hopeless," is used, her behavior probably will be reinforcing that belief. However, if she recognizes that she has "stick-to-it-iveness," a positive concept, she can seek information about her environment and opportunities to confirm that belief. She will look for evidence that she does, in fact, persevere. And when she finds that evidence, her automatic thoughts would be quite different. She would now say to herself things like, "Maybe I can't get anywhere with him now, but if I hang-in-there like I always do, I will eventually get through to him." Such thoughts will lead to continued, task-oriented actions and feelings of power and control. When you think about your environment or your opportunities with a positive belief or attitude, you will find yourself having fewer self-defeating behaviors.

In the next activity, you will examine your basic beliefs and consider others that might be more helpful to you.

Activity 3.5

EXAMINING YOUR BASIC BELIEFS

Goals

1. To help you uncover the basic beliefs you presently attempt to confirm, and

2. to help you utilize other basic beliefs that would be more helpful.

Directions

1. Consider your present basic beliefs. Are you a person that feels hopeless much of the time? Do you catch yourself thinking that there is little you can do that would help you? Do you think that others have more control over what happens to you than you do?

   If any of these descriptions apply to you, then you are using the hopeless/helpless basic belief. Think of how you view situations that confirm that basic belief.

2. Now consider your behavior in general. Look more broadly than the hopeless/helpless beliefs at some positive aspects of your behavior. What basic belief might you hold that would describe your environment and your opportunities within it in realistic ways? Are you a person that keeps trying, no matter what? Are you a "giving" person? Do you possess an "inner strength?"

3. Identify a positive basic belief about yourself that you could use each day. Write that here.

_____

_____

_____

_____

_____

_____

4. Now consider what information you could look for in situations that would confirm this basic belief. For example, what evidence is there that you are a person with "stick-to-it-iveness?" What do you do that demonstrates you have "inner strength" or "personal power?"

5. List here some of these bits of information (Step 4) from situations in which you typically find yourself.

_____

_____

_____

_____

_____

_____

6. Think about how using this positive basic belief about yourself might change your automatic thoughts. What would you now say to yourself in these situations that would help you get through

them without your self-defeating behavior? For example, you might say to yourself, "I have faced this before; I can face it again. The strength I have within can help me remain in-control."

7. Imagine how, by using your positive basic belief from Step 3, you would talk to yourself, and write your automatic thought here.

_____

_____

_____

_____

_____

8. Look at the circle below. You will see how your new basic beliefs, the information you will seek to confirm those beliefs, and automatic thoughts will affect your actions and feelings in ways that will help you overcome your self-defeating behavior.

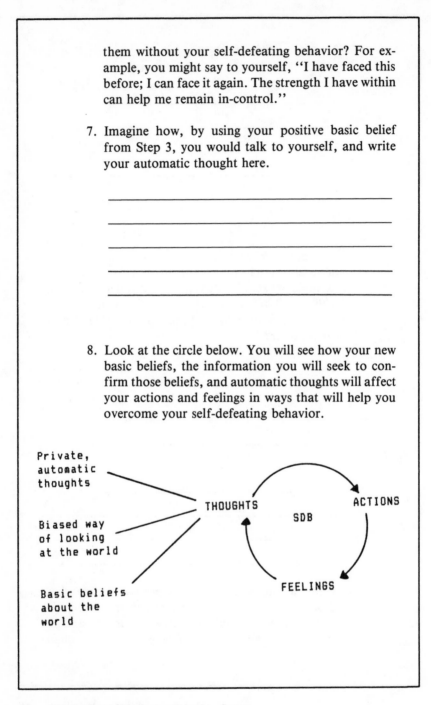

Private, automatic thoughts

Biased way of looking at the world

Basic beliefs about the world

THOUGHTS

SDB

ACTIONS

FEELINGS

Kathy's Response

3. Identify a positive basic belief about yourself that you could use each day. Write that here.

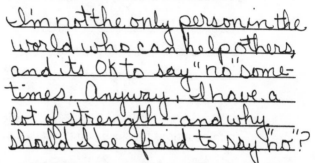

I'm not the only person in the world who can help others, and its OK to say "no" sometimes. Anyway, I have a lot of strength—and why should I be afraid to say "no"?

5. List here some of these bits of information (Step 4) from situations in which you typically find yourself.

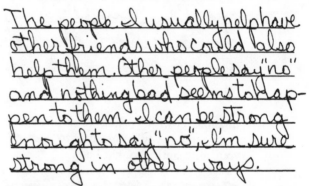

The people I usually help have other friends who could also help them. Other people say "no" and nothing bad seems to happen to them. I can be strong enough to say "no", I'm sure strong in other ways.

7. Imagine how, by using your positive basic belief from Step 3, you would talk to yourself, and write your automatic thought here.

I have a lot of strength, and I will use that to consider my needs first when determining whether or not to help others. I will not feel guilty if I say "no".

Mike's Response

3. Identify a positive basic belief about yourself that you could use each day. Write that here.

I am a hard worker and when I put my mind to it I can accomplish a great deal.

5. List here some of these bits of information (Step 4) from situations in which you typically find yourself.

People compliment me often on my work. I get a lot done and have earned several promotions. I have accomplished some things others find difficult.

7. Imagine how, by using your positive basic belief from Step 3, you would talk to yourself, and write your automatic thought here.

I am a good worker and have contributed a lot to this company. I have ability to do things and have every reason to be successful at most things I try.

Conclusion

As you attempt to change your self-defeating behavior by exiting at the Thoughts Exit, you will find understanding some of the functioning and complexity of the human mind to be helpful. One concept that will contribute to this understanding is the concept of *perception*. Perception is defined as the process through which you become aware of your environment through the organization and interpretation of the evidence of your senses. This means that as raw sensory data are received by your senses they are organized, interpreted and made meaningful to you by your brain. Many factors can influence your perception, including learning and cultural training, states of need and motivation, and your emotional states. For example, the expression "love is blind" suggests that people in love may not see some of the realities of the person with whom they are in love.

Perception is significant in that we all "perceive" our environment in a unique manner. Two different people can be involved in the same situation, yet perceive that situation in very different ways. For example, who is "right" when two friends, or a husband and wife, have an argument? Most arguments involve only one "set of facts," that is, only one reality. Yet each person believes he/she is "right."

What we are suggesting is that human beings have the capacity to "see" and believe what they have been trained, or need, to see and believe. Consequently, your perception of your own behavior, as when you are trying to understand your own self-defeating behavior, is not always objective. Complicating matters further is the fact that this process is often an unconscious one. Thus, staying in touch with reality can be difficult. As you work to understand your own self-defeating behaviors, particularly at the thoughts level, keep in mind that your perception of your behavior and your environment can be easily distorted. An important step toward changing irrational beliefs into rational, productive beliefs is a reasonably accurate perception of reality.

In this unit, you have learned two strategies for eliminating self-defeating behaviors: changing irrational beliefs and changing the way you think about yourself and your environment. Concentrate on using for the time being one or the other of these strategies. Use the one that seems to be best for you. Continue to track the occurrence of your SDBs using the tracking sheets in Unit Two. Work to anticipate your use of your SDBs and be ready to use one of the strategies for exiting the self-defeating circle at the Thoughts Exit.

You will now proceed to Unit Four and consider ways of exiting the self-defeating behavior circle by changing your actions. Changing your actions, in addition to changing your thoughts, will further help you eliminate behaviors that are self-defeating and unproductive.

UNIT **FOUR**

THE ACTIONS EXIT

"Wouldn't it be easier to eliminate my SDB if I had realistic goals?"

Changing thoughts is one way to break out of the self-defeating behavior circle. Now you will be introduced to the Action Exit, which is another way to exit from the SDB circle. This involves setting goals and developing plans to achieve them. The essential task at the Actions Exit is to change inactivity, impulsiveness, or frenzied behavior to goal-oriented, purposeful, and meaningful behavior.

Change From		To
Inactivity	⟶	Goal-oriented action
Impulsiveness	⟶	Purposeful behavior
Frenzied behavior	⟶	Meaningful behavior

The purposes of Unit Four are

1. to identify the actions associated with the problem behavior(s), or SDBs;

2. to develop productive goals designed to eliminate the problem behavior (SDB);

3. to identify the "mini-goals" or steps which lead to your overall goal;

4. to establish a method of evaluating your progress; and

5. to develop and use reinforcements that will help keep you motivated to achieve your goals.

Review of Unit Three

In Unit Three, you learned how to change your thoughts and to change the way you think so as to break out of your SDB circle.

When changing your thoughts you found which of your thoughts were irrational and unproductive and then substituted and challenged them with more rational, productive thoughts. Unproductive thoughts are those loaded with "shoulds, oughts, or musts" and are unsupportable with observable evidence. Productive thoughts, in contrast, are those which can be validated by yourself or by the observations of others.

In Unit Three you also learned to change the way you think by structuring your thinking so that your thoughts become planful, goal oriented, and purposeful. By being planful you avoid being helpless when the conditions which activate your SDB occur.

Examining Your Self-Defeating Actions

Eliminating SDBs at the Actions Exit is an exercise in problem solving with the primary objective of changing unproductive actions into productive actions. Quite frequently people working on problem-solving tasks presume that a problem exists without a thorough analysis of the situation. If the problem cannot be clearly identified and described, however, the work directed towards a solution is meaningless.

Recall that in Unit Two you used the SDB circle to identify the thoughts, actions, and feelings that make-up your problem behavior. You also examined what reinforced your SDB, and you tracked your SDB to determine when and how often it occurs.

Now you will try to become even more specific in terms of identifying the actions associated with your SDB.

Activity 4.1

CLARIFYING YOUR SDB ACTIONS

Goal

To develop a statement that describes you SDB in terms of the actions you take in the situation in which it occurs.

Directions

1. On the SDB Circle below, list your actions that you identified in Unit Two, Activity 2.4.

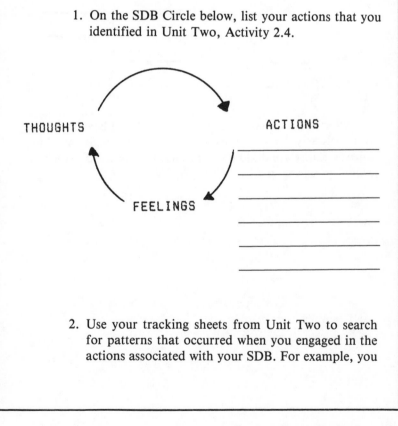

2. Use your tracking sheets from Unit Two to search for patterns that occurred when you engaged in the actions associated with your SDB. For example, you

may have noticed that your SDB occurred more often when you were involved in a particular situation. Write that situation here.

_____

_____

_____

_____

3. Based on a review of your actions and the situations related to your SDB, develop a statement describing more precisely your present SDB actions.

_____

_____

_____

_____

After you have completed Activity 4.1 and have identified more precisely your actions related to your SDB and have reviewed Kathy's and Mike's responses, then proceed to the next section on setting goals.

Kathy's Response

1. On the SDB Circle below, list your actions that you identified in Unit Two, Activity 2.4.

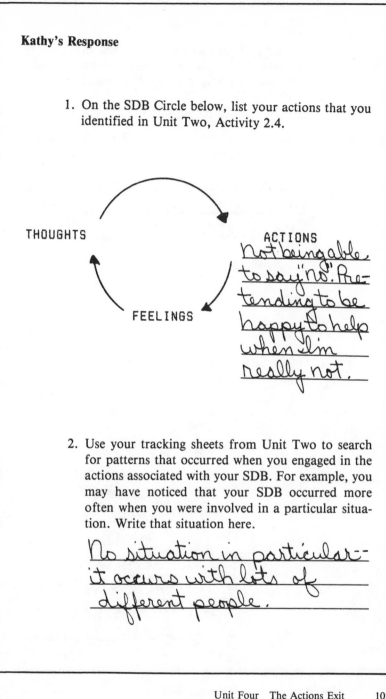

THOUGHTS

ACTIONS

Not being able to say "no". Pretending to be happy to help when I'm really not.

FEELINGS

2. Use your tracking sheets from Unit Two to search for patterns that occurred when you engaged in the actions associated with your SDB. For example, you may have noticed that your SDB occurred more often when you were involved in a particular situation. Write that situation here.

No situation in particular -- it occurs with lots of different people.

3. Based on a review of your actions and the situations related to your SDB, develop a statement describing more precisely your present SDB actions.

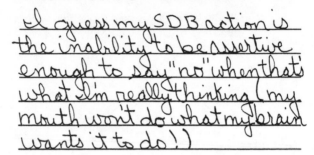

I guess my SDB action is the inability to be assertive enough to say "no" when that's what I'm really thinking (my mouth won't do what my brain wants it to do!)

Mike's Response

1. On the SDB Circle below, list your actions that you identified in Unit Two, Activity 2.4.

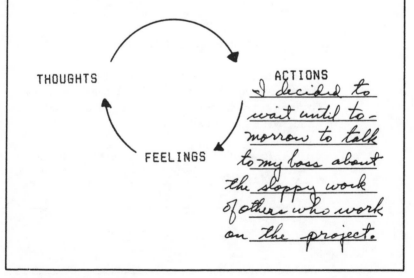

THOUGHTS

ACTIONS
I decided to wait until tomorrow to talk to my boss about the sloppy work of others who work on the project.

FEELINGS

2. Use your tracking sheets from Unit Two to search for patterns that occurred when you engaged in the actions associated with your SDB. For example, you may have noticed that your SDB occurred more often when you were involved in a particular situation. Write that situation here.

When I need to talk to my boss about a problem related to work.

3. Based on a review of your actions and the situations related to your SDB, develop a statement describing more precisely your present SDB actions.

When I need to talk to my boss about a problem involving the job, I get anxious and put off talking to him.

Developing Productive Goals

Quite frequently people are unable to change their behavior because they either have no goals or their goals are vague and unmeasureable. Productive goals are specific statements about the outcomes you expect of yourself. They are written so that they can be measured; that is, you or someone else will actually be able to observe you as you accomplish your goal.

Goal setting is a skill to be developed through practice and following certain rules. Eight rules that will help you be successful when setting goals follow.

Rule #1. Make your goal achievable. Make sure you have enough time and the necessary skills, strengths, abilities, and resources to achieve the goal. An example of an achievable goal is, "Tonight I will do the homework that is due tomorrow in algebra class." An unachievable goal might be "I'll spend five minutes tonight completing the extensive homework due tomorrow in algebra class."

Rule #2. Make sure you can believe in your goal. Your goal must seem realistic to you. You would be unable to believe you could do your algebra homework if you were unable to understand the algebra material. If you understood the material, however, believing in that goal would be an easy thing to do.

Rule #3. Make your goal specific and measurable. If your accomplishment can be observed, counted, or recognized by you or others, then it is measurable. An example of a specific and measurable goal is, "Tonight I will complete the first 10 questions on page 47 of the algebra text." A non-specific goal, on the other hand, would be, "I'll do as much as I can of the algebra class homework sometime today."

Rule #4. Make sure you *want* to achieve your goal. Don't try to reach a goal because you think you "should, ought to, or must." It is better to have algebra class homework as a goal because you want to be prepared for the next class than because you "ought to stay with the teacher's schedule."

Rule #5. Make sure your goal has focus and does not have an alternative. If you set more than one goal, you can distract yourself or divide your energy. An example of a goal with a focus is, "Tonight I will complete the first 10 questions in Chapter 7 of the algebra text." A goal without focus would be, "Tonight I'll either work on algebra or I'll do my psychology class homework. I'll wait to see what I feel like doing." The likelihood of achieving a goal using this last statement is very small because it includes an alternative and thus is distracting.

Rule #6. Try to develop a feeling of motivation. If you are motivated to achieve your goal (that is, if you recognize in advance the benefits you'll have when you achieve your goal), you will have a better chance of reaching your goal. It is motivating to say to yourself, "There is a pay-off in doing the algebra class homework tonight—I'll have less studying to do next week before the test!" On the other hand, you will not help yourself achieve your goal if you say to yourself, "I don't know why I have to do this homework—it seems so silly to study algebra!"

Rule #7. Make sure you have specific dates set for achieving the "minigoals" (or "steps") leading to your goal. If your overall goal is to earn a particular grade on the next algebra test, then one minigoal could be, "I will complete the first 10 algebra problems from Chapter 7 tonight." Your next minigoal might be, "I will complete the last 10 problems from Chapter 7 tomorrow night." It would be a mistake to simply say to yourself, "Somehow I have to complete 20 algebra problems before that next test!"

Rule #8. Make sure you have an idea of the reinforcers (or rewards) you will give yourself as you accomplish your minigoals. If you have a list of rewards from which you can select one reward each time you achieve a minigoal, you will be helping to motivate yourself toward your goal. If, on the other hand, you give yourself no rewards until you finally achieve your goal, you may set yourself up for frustration, instead.

You will use these rules in the next activity as you try to describe your goal as best you can.

Activity 4.2

DEVELOPING A GOAL STATEMENT

Goal

To write a goal statement that is achievable, believable, specific, measurable, and focused.

Directions

1. Read the problem statement that you developed at the end of Activity 4.1 and ask yourself, "How is that different from how I want to be?" By answering this question, you are helping yourself write a "believable" goal.

2. On the lines below, describe how you want to be.

   _____

   _____

   _____

   _____

   _____

   _____

3. Now consider the time, skills, strengths, abilities, and resources necessary to become the way you want to be. Do you have the time to become this way? Do

you have the necessary skills? What strengths, abilities, or resources will you need? Do you have them? By answering these questions, you are helping yourself write an "achievable" goal.

4. If, after considering these things, you do not think you could achieve what you have written in Step 2, modify your description of how you want to be so that it is achievable. Write the modified description below.

_____

_____

_____

_____

_____

5. Examine your preceding description in Step 2 or 4 to determine if it is specific and measurable. Here are some examples of specific and measurable statements.

a. I want to relax 3 times each day for 10 minutes each time.
b. I want to lose 20 pounds by the end of this year.
c. I want to be more organized, and I will begin by cleaning and organizing my desk and bookshelf today.

By making your statement resemble these three examples, you are helping yourself write a "specific and measurable" goal.

6. If you can improve your description in Step 2 or 4 by making it more specific and measurable, write your improved description here.

_____

_____

_____

_____

_____

_____

_____

7. Now examine your description to see if you have described *one way* or *several ways* that you want to be. Make sure that you are describing *only one way* you want to be. By doing this, you are helping yourself write a "focused" goal. While you might like to give yourself alternatives (for example, "I want to be more organized, but I'll settle with being neat"), alternatives decrease the chances of meeting goals. Giving yourself a "second-best" goal is a mistake.

8. If you must rewrite your statement so that it is written as a single goal, do that here.

_____

_____

_____

_____

9. As another important step in this process, examine your statement to see if it is a goal that you believe in, that you want to achieve, and that you know will benefit you. By doing this, you are helping yourself feel "motivated" to reach your goal. If you can honestly say these things about your last statement, then you have written a fine goal statement. If not, modify it as necessary on the lines below.

_____

_____

_____

_____

Kathy's Response

2. On the lines below, describe how you want to be.

I would like to be able to say "no" to people when that's what I'm really thinking, without offending them or having them feel that I won't help them some other time. I'd like to do this without feeling guilty.

4. If, after considering these things, you do not think you could achieve what you have written in Step 2, modify your description of how you want to be so

that it is achievable. Write the modified description below.

I think I have the ability to accomplish this goal-- I just have to develop the courage to try a new behavior for me.

6. If you can improve your description in Step 2 or 4 by making it more specific and measurable, write your improved description here.

Each time someone asks me for help, I will think of my needs, such as my time and desire to help, and will weigh my needs against how important the other person's problem is and whether or not there is someone else who could help.

8. If you must rewrite your statement so that it is written as a single goal, do that here.

I think it's OK.

9. As another important step in this process, examine your statement to see if it is a goal that you believe in, that you want to achieve, and that you know will benefit you. By doing this, you are helping yourself feel "motivated" to reach your goal. If you can honestly say these things about your last statement,

then you have written a fine goal statement. If not, modify it as necessary on the lines below.

_OK_

Mike's Response

2. On the lines below, describe how you want to be.

I want to be able to talk to my boss about problems related to the job without procrastinating.

4. If, after considering these things, you do not think you could achieve what you have written in Step 2, modify your description of how you want to be so that it is achievable. Write the modified description below.

I believe I could achieve what I have written above.

6. If you can improve your description in Step 2 or 4 by making it more specific and measurable, write your improved description here.

I want to be able to discuss problems with my boss related to our current project on a regular basis if necessary. To discuss problems no more than 24 hours after they occur.

8. If you must rewrite your statement so that it is written as a single goal, do that here.

   It's O.K. as is.

9. As another important step in this process, examine your statement to see if it is a goal that you believe in, that you want to achieve, and that you know will benefit you. By doing this, you are helping yourself feel "motivated" to reach your goal. If you can honestly say these things about your last statement, then you have written a fine goal statement. If not, modify it as necessary on the lines below.

   It's O.K. as is.

Identifying Your Minigoals

In order to take the productive actions that lead to your goal, an extremely helpful procedure is to break the goal into "minigoals." Minigoals are steps that are sequential and build on each other. They are like a blueprint, in that they outline what needs to be done each step of the way from the unproductive actions you use today to the productive actions you wish to use in the future.

Earlier in this Unit, an example was used in which the goal was the achievement of a particular grade on an algebra test. A well-written goal, such as, "I want to achieve a grade of 'B' on next Friday's algebra test," might have the following minigoals:

"I will complete the first 10 problems in Chapter 7 tonight."

"I will speak with Dr. Smith after class tomorrow to determine if my solutions are correct."

"I will complete the last 10 problems in Chapter 7 tomorrow night."

"I will make an appointment with Dr. Smith so that I can examine the 20 problems and my solutions with her on Friday."

"By Monday, I will have outlined the major points of Chapter 7 in my notebook."

"Tuesday evening, Judy and I will quiz each other orally about the major points of Chapter 7."

"Wednesday evening, I will attempt 10 of the 'Extra Problems' in Chapter 7. If I can get 8 of them correct, I will be prepared to earn a 'B' on Friday's test. If I get fewer than 8 correct, I will see Dr. Smith on Thursday."

In the preceding activities, you described the actions that are causing you problems and the goal that you want to reach. Next you will develop a plan for reaching that goal by outlining the mini-goals that you will need to accomplish along the way.

Activity 4.3

LISTING YOUR MINIGOALS

Goal

To enable you to identify the steps you will need to accomplish as you progress toward your goal.

Directions

1. Read once again your description at the end of Activity 4.1 of your present actions.

2. Read your description at the end of Activity 4.2 of your goal.

3. Now make a list of all the possible steps that will help you achieve your goal. You have room below for up to 10 steps. Don't be concerned about the order in which these steps should be taken.

   Example:

         Goal: "I want to change jobs."

         Steps: a. Examine the newspaper want-ads.
                b. Contact the employment service.
                c. Update my resume.

   a. _____

   b. _____

   c. _____

d. _____

e. _____

f. _____

g. _____

h. _____

i. _____

j. _____

4. Now prioritize your list. In prioritizing your list, you will be establishing "minigoals" that you need to achieve as you make progress toward your goal. Put your steps in order from 1 to 10 (or fewer as needed).

Minigoal   1._____

Minigoal   2._____

Minigoal   3._____

Minigoal   4._____

Minigoal   5._____

Minigoal   6._____

Minigoal   7._____

Minigoal   8._____

Minigoal   9._____

Minigoal 10._____

5. Design an "Action Plan" by entering your minigoals and goal on the following diagram. This plan is quite special. Like a roadmap, it gives you specific directions for achieving your goal. And, like a guage, it

allows you to measure your progress so that you can modify your plan if and when that becomes necessary.

Now complete the diagram by transposing your prioritized list (Step 4) onto that chart. Use as many of the "minigoal" boxes as you need.

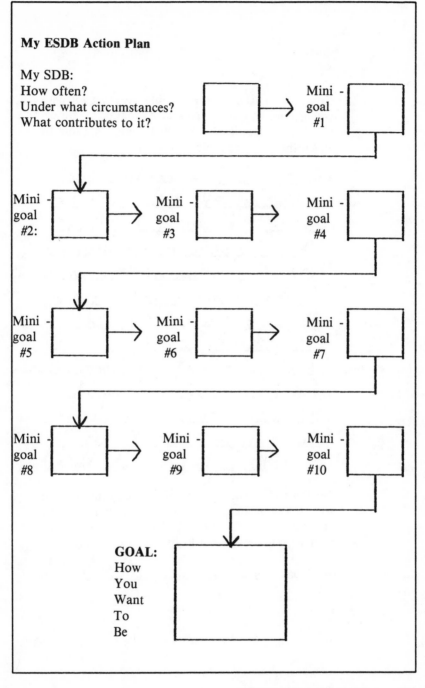

My ESDB Action Plan

My SDB:
How often?
Under what circumstances?
What contributes to it?

Mini - goal #1

Mini - goal #2:

Mini - goal #3

Mini - goal #4

Mini - goal #5

Mini - goal #6

Mini - goal #7

Mini - goal #8

Mini - goal #9

Mini - goal #10

GOAL:
How
You
Want
To
Be

Kathy's Response

3. Now make a list of all the possible steps that will help you achieve your goal. You have room below for up to 10 steps. Don't be concerned about the order in which these steps should be taken.

a. Ask myself if I have time to help.

b. Ask myself if what I want to do is really important to me.

c. Ask the other person how urgent his/her problem is.

d. Ask the other person if there is anyone else who could help him/her.

e. Ask if I might help at another time.

f. Politely decline to help if I really feel I don't have the time or don't want to help considering the circumstances.

4. Now prioritize your list. In prioritizing your list, you will be establishing "minigoals" that you need to achieve as you make progress toward your goal. Put your steps in order from 1 to 10 (or fewer as needed).

Minigoal 1. I think they're OK as listed.

5. Design an "Action Plan" by entering your minigoals and goal on the following diagram. This plan is quite special. Like a roadmap, it gives you specific directions for achieving your goal. And, like a gauge, it allows you to measure your progress so that you can modify your plan if and when that become necessary.

Now complete the diagram by transposing your prioritized list (Step 4) onto that chart. Use as many of the "minigoal" boxes as you need.

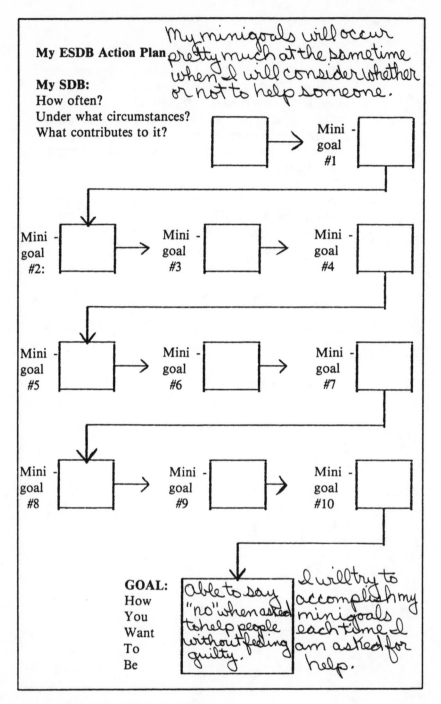

My ESDB Action Plan *My minigoals will occur pretty much at the same time when I will consider whether or not to help someone.*

My SDB:
How often?
Under what circumstances?
What contributes to it?

Mini - goal #1

Mini - goal #2:

Mini - goal #3

Mini - goal #4

Mini - goal #5

Mini - goal #6

Mini - goal #7

Mini - goal #8

Mini - goal #9

Mini - goal #10

GOAL:
How
You
Want
To
Be

Able to say "no" when asked to help people without feeling guilty.

I will try to accomplish my minigoals each time I am asked for help.

Mike's Response

3. Now make a list of all the possible steps that will help you achieve your goal. You have room below for up to 10 steps. Don't be concerned about the order in which these steps should be taken.

a. _Rehearse what I will say to my boss._

b. _Write a brief description of the problems as I see them._

c. _Talk with my friend Bill to see if I am not exaggerating._

d. _Talk to my boss about positive things to get used to talking to him._

e. _Track the problems when they occur so I can be specific._

f. _Use Ellis' model to check out irrational thoughts._

g. _Find out when my boss has time to talk without interruption._

h. _Set a specific time to talk to my boss._

i. _Develop a "Plan B" in case this doesn't work._

j. _Decide how I am to reward myself after accomplishing each step._

4. Now prioritize your list. In prioritizing your list, you will be establishing "minigoals" that you need to achieve as you make progress toward your goal. Put your steps in order from 1 to 10 (or fewer as needed).

Minigoal 1. _Write a brief description of the problems as I see them._

Minigoal 2. _Check them out with my friend Bill._

Minigoal 3. _Track the problems as to when they occur._

Minigoal 4. _Find out when my boss has time to talk._

Minigoal 5. _Set a specific time to talk with him._

Minigoal 6. _Rehearse what I will say._

Minigoal 7. _Use Ellis' model to check out irrational thoughts_

Minigoal 8. _Develop a "Plan B."_

Minigoal 9. _Talk to my boss about positive things._

Minigoal 10. _Talk to my boss about the problems as I see them and reward myself for each step accomplished._

5. Design an "Action Plan" by entering your minigoals and goal on the following diagram. This plan is quite special. Like a roadmap, it gives you specific directions for achieving your goal. And, like a gauge, it allows you to measure your progress so that you can modify your plan if and when that becomes necessary.

Now complete the diagram by transposing your prioritized list (Step 4) onto that chart. Use as many of the "minigoal" boxes as you need.

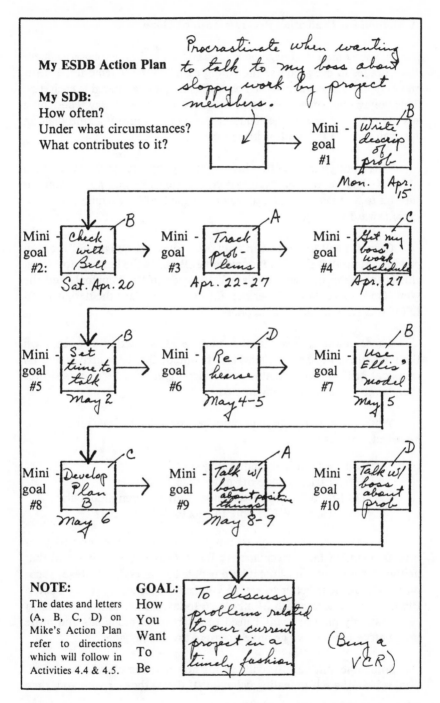

My ESDB Action Plan

My SDB:
How often?
Under what circumstances?
What contributes to it?

Procrastinate when wanting to talk to my boss about sloppy work by project members.

Mini - goal #1 — *Write descrip of prob* B

Mon. | *Apr. 15*

Mini - goal #2: — *Check with Bill* B
Sat. Apr. 20

Mini - goal #3 — *Track prob-lems* A
Apr. 22-27

Mini - goal #4 — *Get my boss' work schedule* C
Apr. 27

Mini - goal #5 — *Set time to talk* B
May 2

Mini - goal #6 — *Re-hearse* D
May 4-5

Mini - goal #7 — *Use Ellis' model* B
May 5

Mini - goal #8 — *Develop Plan B* C
May 6

Mini - goal #9 — *Talk w/ boss about positive things* A
May 8-9

Mini - goal #10 — *Talk w/ boss about prob* D

NOTE:
The dates and letters (A, B, C, D) on Mike's Action Plan refer to directions which will follow in Activities 4.4 & 4.5.

GOAL:
How
You
Want
To
Be

To discuss problems related to our current project in a timely fashion

(Buy a VCR)

A Method for Evaluating Progress Toward Goals

A young man in college once prepared an elaborate plan to achieve "A" grades in every course the young man took that semester. Unfortunately, he was never satisfied with his plan, so he altered it each day. This young man spent significant amounts of time each day redesigning his plan. By the end of the semester, he had a beautiful action plan on his wall, and "Fs" in all of his courses.

This young man's difficulties went beyond the development of a plan. He had never completed two crucial steps: he had not committed himself to his plan nor had he developed a method for evaluating his progress toward his goals.

Commitment to a plan can only occur once the designer of the plan can be certain that the plan is achievable. Perhaps the best way of doing this is to establish "deadline dates" for each of the minigoals and the goal. Once those dates are written on the action plan, the designer can tell if it is truly an achievable plan.

Those dates serve yet another purpose. Once action has begun on the plan, the dates become markers. If one of the dates arrives and its minigoal has not been completed, then progress on the plan is slower than what was originally anticipated.

When this occurs, the plan must be reevaluated. Questions need to be asked, such as

"Did I establish enough minigoals?"
"Have I tried to bite off more than I can chew?"
"Do I need to give myself more time between minigoals?"
"Now when will I be able to accomplish my goal?"

No reason exists for you to punish yourself for not meeting your original plan. In fact, psychiatrist William Glasser (1975) has said that neither excuses nor punishment help people be successful. Instead, focus on your plan. It is better to say to yourself, "According to my Action Plan, I was to accomplish Minigoal #6 today. I have not. Now I must reexamine my plan to see if I need to insert more minigoals and more time before I can make genuine progress toward my goal."

Sometimes one has difficulty seeing how inaction (that is, lack of action) is part of a self-defeating behavior. If that is the case with you, then simply acting in any way may help you break out of your self-defeating behaviors. Remember, your reluctance to act in the past may have been caused by failed attempts to achieve a goal in one giant step. As has been pointed out in this Unit, several successive steps increasing in difficulty will ultimately get you to your goal. A first step may simply be to act—to do anything which will help you to "get into gear" rather than be hopelessly stuck.

Some psychologists, like Dr. Merle Ohlsen at Indiana State University (1977, 1983), believe that setting goals and minigoals, working toward them, and evaluating your progress is a very important process which must be taught to people to help them overcome any self-defeating behavior.

In the next activity, you will set-up your action plan so that you can evaluate your progress toward your goal.

Activity 4.4

EVALUATING YOUR PROGRESS

Goal

To complete your action plan by establishing target dates for your minigoals and goals.

Directions

1. Return to the last page of Activity 4.3 and, below each box in which you have written a minigoal, write the date when you believe you will have successfully completed that goal.

2. Now do the same thing for your goal as described on the last page of Activity 4.3. By what date do you think you can achieve your goal?

3. As you progress through your plan, check your Action Plan to see if you are "on schedule" as you complete minigoals.

4. If you are behind your original schedule, determine if you need more minigoals or if you need to lengthen the time between your minigoals. Regardless of the reason, you will need to change the date on which you will be able to achieve your goal.

5. Periodically reexamine your Action Plan. You always will be able to evaluate your progress toward your goal.

Effective Use of Reinforcements

People are often good at planning rewards they will give themselves once they reach major goals. Some people promise to buy themselves some new clothes once they lose 20 pounds. Others promise themselves a vacation once they successfully complete a project at work.

While such rewards may seem at first glance to be sensible uses of reinforcements, they are not as effective as they could be because they do not happen soon enough. In order to motivate people toward reaching goals, they must be rewarded every step of the way.

Effective use of reinforcements requires that you develop "mini-reinforcers" that you can give yourself as you reach each of your minigoals. It is a good idea to plan a major reward that you can get once you achieve the goal, too.

Earlier in this Unit, goals and minigoals were described using the achievement of a "B" grade on an algebra test as an example. Assume for a moment that the person in that example loved watching television programs in the evening. A "mini-reinforcer" for reaching each of those minigoals could be watching an hour of television each night. That reinforcer would be given only if the minigoal for that day was achieved. Otherwise, there would be no TV-watching until the next minigoal was achieved!

If you recall from Unit Two, reinforcers are anything that increase the chances of your repeating the action you just took. More specifically, reinforcers are those things you find pleasant. Determining what is pleasant for you, then, is the first step in using reinforcers effectively.

In the next activity, you will identify ways in which you can reward yourself for progressing toward your goal.

Activity 4.5

DEVELOPING USEFUL REINFORCERS

Goal

To enable you to identify pleasant ways you can reward yourself for moving towards your goals. A reward may be something as simple as taking a walk or more involved like taking a vacation.

Directions:

1. Below, list some small things you enjoy.

    a. _____

    b. _____

    c. _____

    d. _____

2. Now list several major events that you find especially rewarding.

    a. _____

    b. _____

    c. _____

    d. _____

3. Identify how you can use these pleasant activities as rewards for progressing through your action plan.

To do so, return to your Action Plan at the end of Activity 4.3 and after each minigoal, write a letter that represents one of the "small pleasures" you listed in Step 1. After the goal, write a letter that represents one of the "major events" you listed in Step 2.

As you progress through your Action Plan, be sure to give yourself the reinforcer you just listed on the plan. As you do that, you'll motivate yourself to reach your goal.

4. Give yourself the reinforcer *only* if and when you accomplished that particular minigoal. No minigoal, no reinforcer!

Kathy's Response

1. Below, list some small things you enjoy.

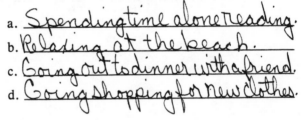

a. Spending time alone reading.
b. Relaxing at the beach.
c. Going out to dinner with a friend.
d. Going shopping for new clothes.

2. Now list several major events that you find especially rewarding.

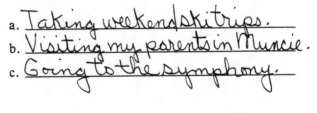

a. Taking weekend ski trips.
b. Visiting my parents in Muncie.
c. Going to the symphony.

Mike's Response

1. **Below, list some small things you enjoy.**

   a. <u>Reading mystery stories.</u>
   b. <u>Ice Cream</u>
   c. <u>A drive in the country</u>
   d. <u>Going to a baseball game.</u>

2. Now list several major events that you find especially rewarding.

   a. <u>Going to the beach for a few days.</u>
   b. <u>Buying a new suit.</u>
   c. <u>Going to a play.</u>
   d. <u>Buying a VCR</u>

Conclusion

The Actions Exit strategies involve (1) becoming more goal-oriented, (2) setting-up actions so that you can succeed, and (3) rewarding yourself with pleasant activities as you successfully progress toward your goals. As you consider what actions you can take to eliminate your self-defeating behaviors, try to use these "ingredients." We think that you will surprise yourself with the ease at which you can short-circuit self-defeating behaviors by taking appropriate actions.

In the next unit, you will learn how your *feelings* can help you "break-out" of self-defeating behaviors.

UNIT **FIVE**

THE FEELINGS EXIT

"How can I use my feelings to eliminate my self-defeating behavior?"

At this point, you have learned strategies for changing your thoughts and actions in order to lessen self-defeating behaviors. But what about the feelings you have when you engage in your SDB? How can they be used to help you exit from the self-defeating behavior circle?

The purposes of Unit Five are

1. to help you identify feelings associated with your SDB;

2. to enable you to use your feelings as a signal that you are engaging in your SDB;

3. to help you create positive feelings within yourself, such as calmness, that are incompatible with your SDB; and

4. to help you modify your feelings so they are more appropriate for the situations in which you are.

Review of Unit Four

In the last unit, you learned how to set goals and minigoals in order to act more productively. You closely examined your target SDB and developed action-oriented goals and minigoals to exit your SDB circle. You considered issues such as how to effectively reinforce yourself for moving through your action plan, and how to evaluate progress toward your goal. In general, you learned how you could benefit from your behavior becoming more planful and purposeful.

Feelings and SDBs

According to Ellis and Harper (1975), feelings are the consequences of irrational thinking. The ESDB System demonstrates that feelings also *contribute* to the creation and maintenance of SDBs. Consider, once again, the SDB Circle:

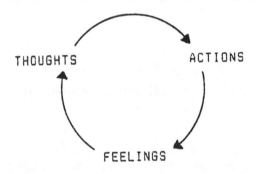

THOUGHTS   ACTIONS

FEELINGS

The thoughts you have, and the actions you take, as you engage in your SDB seem to lead almost automatically to feelings. Just as your thoughts and actions can be unproductive, your feelings can be unproductive, too. Very often, the feelings associated with your SDB are "blown out of proportion" to the event actually occurring. Such unproductive feelings lead to more unproductive thoughts and actions. On and on the SDB circle goes, until eventually your self-defeating behavior becomes "stamped-in."

As an example, think of people you know who appear excessively anxious much of the time. Have you noticed that they often appear easily excitable, troubled, confused, unable to make decisions, or incapable of using time effectively? It is as if their self-defeating behavior, such as an inability to make decisions, allows them to control their anxiety! In reality, of course, the SDB does not help them. Instead, the SDB may simply help these people avoid the situation in which they are anxious (an example of negative reinforcement "stamping-in" the SDB). A self-defeating behavior, therefore, is something which people use to handle or cope with a feeling such as anxiety, but it only provides short-term relief.

The next activity is designed to help you understand better how some of your feelings may be the result of, or contribute to, your self-defeating behaviors.

Activity 5.1

IDENTIFYING YOUR SDB FEELINGS

Goal

To identify the feelings you have before, during, and after your SDB.

Directions

1. On the SDB Circle below, list your feelings that you identified in Unit Two, Activity 2.4.

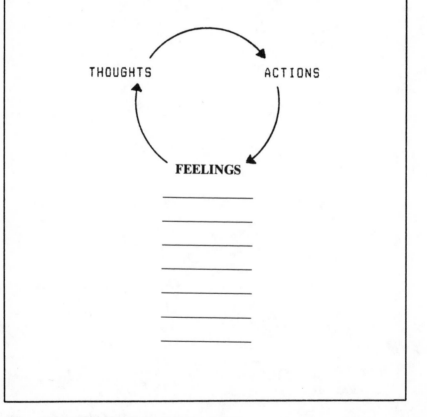

THOUGHTS   ACTIONS

FEELINGS

2. Recall which of these feelings you have *just before* you engage in your SDB.

   Example: Fear, jitteriness, rapid heartbeat, "butterflies" in my stomach.

   Your Feelings:_____

   _____

   _____

   _____

3. Recall what feelings you have *while* you engage in your SDB:

   Example: Panic, very agitated, "pumped up"

   Your Feelings:_____

   _____

   _____

   _____

4. Recall what feelings you have *just after* you engage in your SDB.

   Example: Relief, tired

   Your Feelings:_____

   _____

   _____

   _____

5. Now try to "evaluate" these feelings. Do they *typically* occur when you engage in your SDB? Are they *appropriate* to the situation in which you are at the time? Are they *blown out of proportion?* Do you think they *block you* from reaching your goals? Write your evaluation of your feelings, before, during, and after your SDB here.

_____

_____

_____

_____

_____

_____

_____

Understanding the feelings associated with your SDBs is valuable. You can use this understanding to uncover "warning signs" which occur just prior to engaging in your SDB. That's the subject of the next section. Notice that some of your feelings are physical (bodily feelings) and some are emotional. Both can serve as "SDB cues."

Kathy's Response

1. On the SDB Circle below, list your feelings that you identified in Unit Two, Activity 2.4.

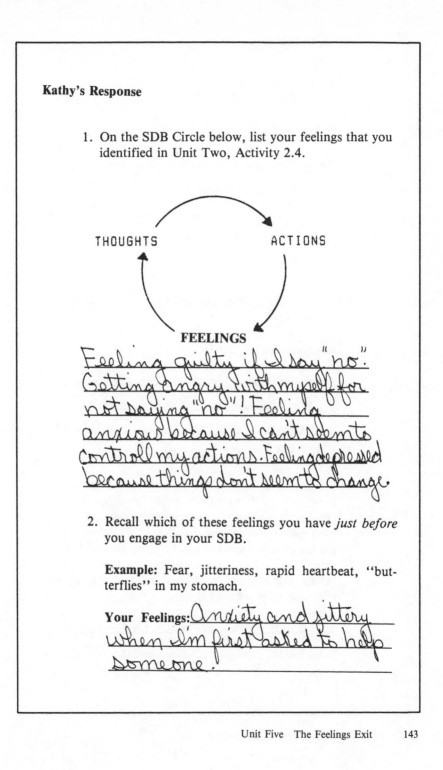

THOUGHTS

ACTIONS

FEELINGS

Feeling guilty if I say "no".
Getting angry with myself for
not saying "no"! Feeling
anxious because I can't seem to
control my actions. Feeling depressed
because things don't seem to change.

2. Recall which of these feelings you have *just before* you engage in your SDB.

Example: Fear, jitteriness, rapid heartbeat, "butterflies" in my stomach.

Your Feelings: Anxiety and jittery
when I'm first asked to help
someone.

3. Recall what feelings you have *while* you engage in your SDB:

Example: Panic, very agitated, "pumped up"

Your Feelings: Guilty if I say "no" and anxious because I'm not able to control the situation.

4. Recall what feelings you have *just after* you engage in your SDB.

Example: Relief, tired

Your Feelings: Angry at self for not saying "no" and depressed because I can't seem to change.

5. Now try to "evaluate" these feelings. Do they *typically* occur when you engage in your SDB? Are they *appropriate* to the situation in which you are at the time? Are they *blown out of proportion?* Do you think they *block you* from reaching your goals? Write your evaluation of your feelings, before, during, and after your SDB here.

I probably shouldn't feel guilty just for saying "no".

sometimes. Being anxious and nervous reflects my lack of control and they would probably go away if I were more assertive, as would my depression and anger.

Mike's Response

1. On the SDB Circle below, list your feelings that you identified in Unit Two, Activity 2.4.

THOUGHTS   ACTIONS

FEELINGS

Butterflies in my stomach.
Sweating
Anxious --
heart pounds.

2. Recall which of these feelings you have *just before* you engage in your SDB.

Example: Fear, jitteriness, rapid heartbeat, "butterflies" in my stomach.

Your Feelings: *Butterflies, dry mouth -- can't seem to get words out right.*

3. Recall what feelings you have *while* you engage in your SDB:

Example: Panic, very agitated, "pumped up"

Your Feelings: *Excited, afraid, scared, nervous*

4. Recall what feelings you have *just after* you engage in your SDB.

Example: Relief, tired

Your Feelings: *Disappointment, frustration, embarrassed.*

5. Now try to "evaluate" these feelings. Do they *typically* occur when you engage in your SDB? Are they *appropriate* to the situation in which you are at the time? Are they *blown out of proportion?* Do you think they *block you* from reaching your goals? Write your evaluation of your feelings, before, during, and after your SDB here.

They usually occur when I want to talk to my boss about the sloppy work of others. It's silly because my boss is easy to approach and my feelings probably are realistic in terms of consequences of pointing out problems to my boss.

SDB Cues

Without realizing it some physical sensations may occur within you that immediately precede your self-defeating behavior. These physical sensations, or "SDB cues," can be a great aid in exiting from the SDB Circle at the Feelings Exit.

Gunnison (1976) and Cerio (1983) found this in college students. For example, people with "test-anxiety" often have a racing heartbeat, sweaty palms, a "knot-in-the-stomach," or an eye-twitch *just before* they panic during tests. When this "flight into panic" (Gunnison, 1976) appears, the result often is the "blanking-out" on tests.

Using what you learned in the previous section, and considering the notion that an emotional "cue" precedes your SDB, perhaps you could design a method for doing away with an SDB. That is precisely what Gunnison (1976) proposed.

In the Fantasy Relaxation Technique (Gunnison, 1976; Cerio, 1983), systematic relaxation, the countdown of numbers, and imagery are used to teach people how to (1) relax, (2) identify their physical cue, and (3) relax quickly once the physical cue is noticed. If you can do these three things, you would be "short-circuiting" your SDB from ever occurring.

In the references for this book are listed papers (Gunnison, 1976; Cerio, 1983) that explain the Fantasy Relaxation Technique (FRT). You can learn how to use FRT by reading these papers, although we recommend that if you intend to make extensive use of it that you receive formal training in its use. A counselor or psychologist familiar with FRT can provide you with the best training. We will use some FRT here to help you in eliminating SDBs. Activities 5.2 and 5.3 use FRT concepts and will be helpful to you.

Activity 5.2

THE FANTASY RELAXATION
TECHNIQUE (FRT)—PART 1

Goals

1. To systematically relax yourself and

2. to use three numbers to relax yourself even more.

Directions

1. Sit in a quiet, comfortable place. Allow your mind to wander for a few minutes.

2. Think of your body as being in three sections. "Section 3" is the upper part, and it includes your head, neck, shoulders, arms, and hands. "Section 2" is the middle part, including your chest, back stomach, and abdomen. "Section 1" is the lower part, including your hips, buttocks, legs, ankles, and feet.

3. Tense, hold, and then relax the muscles in Section 3. First do the muscles in your face. Then do your neck muscles. Next, do your shoulders. Now tense and relax the muscles in your arms. Finally, tense and relax the muscles in your hands and fingers. Notice how Section 3 seems more settled, loose, and calm after tensing and relaxing the muscles in it.

4. Now tense, hold, and then relax the muscles in Section 2. First do this to your back. Next, allow your breathing to take place at a comfortable pace. Now tense your stomach and abdomen, and relax both. Notice how relaxed Section 2 feels. In fact, the only part of your body which may still seem "jittery" is Section 1.

5. Now it's time to tense, hold, and relax the muscles in Section 1. First tense your buttocks and hips. Now relax them. Next, tense your leg muscles. Relax those. Finally, tense your feet and toes. As you relax your feet and toes, you're relaxing the last of the muscles in Section 1. Your entire body should be relaxed by now.

6. With your eyes closed, try to visualize Sections 3, 2, and 1.

7. Now, say softly, "3." When you say "3," you also should visualize Section 3 and let the muscles in it relax as much as possible.

8. Repeat Step 7, but for Section 2. Say "2" softly, visualize Section 2, and relax its muscles.

9. Repeat Step 7 again, but this time for Section 1. Be sure to say "1" as you visualize and relax the muscles in Section 1.

10. Now say the three numbers softly, and try to imagine a wave of relaxation going through you from head to toe. Say "3, 2, 1." You may want to repeat this Step several times.

11. Stop whenever you want to. It is a good idea to move slowly in the minute or two following this relaxation training, since your body may need time to adjust to activity after being relaxed.

As with most new things you try to learn, "practice makes perfect." The more often you practice Activity 5.2, the more expert you will become at being able to relax yourself quickly.

Fantasy Relaxation Technique—
Further Application

For many people quick relaxation is enough to short-circuit their SDB. The reason for this appears to be that "panic" is a feeling often experienced as an SDB begins. Because "relaxation" is the opposite feeling from "panic," relaxing yourself seems to inhibit your feeling of panic. Panic is "incompatible" with relaxation. If you do not feel panic, then an important component of your SDB will be missing. You will have exited the SDB Circle at the Feelings Exit.

Although helpful for some people, quick relaxation is not, in itself, sufficient to eliminate their SDBs. That is why FRT goes one step further. In the next activity, you will learn to identify a physical or emotional cue that signals the beginning of your SDB.

Activity 5.3

THE FANTASY RELAXATION TECHNIQUE (FRT)—PART 2

Goal

To identify a physical or emotional cue that signals the beginning of your SDB. You will also learn to use the three-number countdown when you notice your SDB cue.

Directions

1. Practice, if you have not already done so, Activity 5.2 many times. Practice until you can relax by simply counting "3, 2, 1" softly to yourself. Do that now.

2. Once you are deeply relaxed, allow yourself to imagine the last time you engaged in your SDB. Start by imagining the events that preceded the SDB.

3. The moment you have a physical or emotional feeling different from the way you feel while deeply relaxed, stop and write that feeling here.

_____

_____

_____

_____

4. Now, countdown the numbers. Say "3, 2, 1" softly. Continue this until you are deeply relaxed.

5. Repeat Step 2.

6. The moment you have a physical or emotional feeling, stop and write that feeling here.

_____

_____

_____

_____

Once again, countdown until you are deeply relaxed. Say "3, 2, 1."

7. Repeat Step 2 a few more times. Write the feelings here, and then countdown to relax yourself each time.

_____

_____

_____

_____

8. Slowly allow yourself to emerge from your relaxed state. Now examine the feelings you wrote on the lines above. Was any feeling listed more than once? If one was, that feeling is probably your SDB cue.

9. In the future, be on the look-out for your SDB cue. It is a signal that you are about to engage in your

SDB. When you notice the cue, countdown to relax yourself. Each time you do, you will be "short-circuiting" the SDB Circle and decreasing the chances that your SDB will occur again.

Kathy's Response

3. The moment you have a physical or emotional feeling different from the way you feel while deeply relaxed, stop and write that feeling here.

   Guilt and anxiety

6. The moment you have a physical or emotional feeling, stop and write that feeling here.

   Same ones

   Once again, countdown until you are deeply relaxed. Say "3, 2, 1."

7. Repeat Step 2 a few more times. Write the feelings here, and then countdown to relax yourself each time.

   Guilt and anxiety occur most often when I imagine someone asking me to help them and I really don't want to.

Mike's Response

3. The moment you have a physical or emotional feeling different from the way you feel while deeply relaxed, stop and write that feeling here.

Butterflies in my stomach.

6. The moment you have a physical or emotional feeling, stop and write that feeling here.

Afraid

Once again, countdown until you are deeply relaxed. Say "3, 2, 1."

7. Repeat Step 2 a few more times. Write the feelings here, and then countdown to relax yourself each time.

Palms sweat.
Hard to get words out.

When Are Feelings Appropriate?

One reason people have self-defeating behaviors is that they blow an incident out of proportion. They, for example, may think that a particular situation is worse than it really is. Or they may become overly elated when something "great" occurs, only to "crash" later into sadness when the "great event" is over.

When you blow your thoughts out of proportion, feelings are created within you that are inappropriate for the situation in which you find yourself. Such feelings serve to over-sensitize or over-arouse you. Such "over-done" feelings rarely allow you to function at your best levels. When you are not at your best, SDBs can easily occur.

To change feelings is difficult when you are engaged in an SDB. But if you can examine your SDB feelings now, you could gain some valuable insight. If you find evidence of "out-of-proportion" feelings, you could consider what feelings would be more appropriate in that situation. Inevitably, the more appropriate feelings will be associated with lower arousal levels. The lower your arousal, the better are your chances of being more in-control and having fewer SDBs. "An ounce of prevention could be worth a pound of cure!"

Activity 5.4

EVALUATING YOUR FEELINGS

Goals

1. To examine the feelings that occur during your SDB,

2. to consider their appropriateness for the situation, and

3. to consider other feelings that might better fit the situation.

Directions

1. Return to Activity 5.1 and examine the feelings you wrote there. Do any of those feelings seem inappropriate for the situation in which you were?

2. Write here (a) the situation, (b) the feeling you had described in Activity 5.1, and (c) a feeling that you now think would be more appropriate (that is, less arousing) in that situation.

   a. The situation:_____

   _____

   _____

   _____

b. The actual feeling:_____

_____

_____

c. A more appropriate feeling:_____

_____

_____

_____

3. Try this analysis again, but this time for a different situation in which your SDB occurs.

a. The   situation:_____

_____

_____

_____

b. The actual feeling:_____

_____

_____

_____

c. A more appropriate feeling:_____

_____

_____

_____

4. Now consider this: Is there a way that you could cause yourself to have more appropriate feelings in the future? How could you do that? Any ideas that you have should be written here.

_____

_____

_____

_____

You would benefit from returning to this question again and again. The more you can *prepare yourself* for having appropriate feelings, the more you will help yourself eliminate your SDBs.

Kathy's Response

2. Write here (a) the situation, (b) the feeling you had described in Activity 5.1, and (c) a feeling that you now think would be more appropriate (that is, less arousing) in that situation.

a. The situation: *Being asked to help someone.*

b. the actual feeling: *Anxiety.*

c. A more appropriate feeling: *Calmness while I consider my minigoals and analyze the situation.*

3. Try this analysis again, but this time for a different situation in which your SDB occurs.

    a. The situation: _The same--being asked for help._

    b. the actual feeling: _Guilt_

    c. A more appropriate feeling: _I don't have to help everyone all the time and I don't need to feel so guilty for saying "no"._

4. Now consider this: Is there a way that you could cause yourself to have more appropriate feelings in the future? How could you do that? Any ideas that you have should be written here.

    As I wrote earlier--I think I need to work most on not feeling so guilty and being so anxious. I think if I just try saying "no" sometimes it will help a lot.

Mike's Response

2. Write here (a) the situation, (b) the feeling you had described in Activity 5.1, and (c) a feeling that you now think would be more appropriate (that is, less arousing) in that situation.

a. The situation: *When I go to talk to my boss about sloppy work by others on the project I get butterflies.*

b. The actual feeling: *Butterflies in my stomach. I feel like I could throw-up.*

c. A more appropriate feeling: *Some anxiousness, but only enough to help me be effective when describing problems to my boss.*

3. Try this analysis again, but this time for a different situation in which your SDB occurs.

a. The situation: *I procrastinate about asking my neighbors*

to stop parking in front
of my mailbox.

b. the actual feeling: _Get anxious_
because I think this will
lead to an unpleasant
confrontation and argument.

c. A more appropriate feeling: _I may be_
a little anxious, but if
I am to change the situation
I need to be assertive --
it will be worth it.

4. Now consider this: Is there a way that you could
   cause yourself to have more appropriate feelings in
   the future? How could you do that? Any ideas that
   you have should be written here.

Check out my perceptions
with a friend to be sure the
problem isn't exaggerated.
Rehearse when I have to say
something difficult to someone.

Conclusion

In Unit Five, you have learned methods for relaxing, for "short-circuiting" SDBs, and for considering the appropriateness of your feelings. Throughout this book, you have been examining the three SDB exits quite thoroughly. Yet two questions still seem to remain unanswered:

1. How might all that you have learned to eliminate SDBs *fail you?* In other words, how might your fine efforts go awry?

2. What thoughts, actions, and feelings will help you behave in *self-enhancing ways* in the future?

These two questions will be addressed in the next unit.

UNIT **SIX**

TOWARD SELF-ENHANCING BEHAVIORS

"How can I use the ESDB System to become happier and more productive?"

Think of the strategies you have learned to eliminate self-defeating behaviors as skills much like those involved in solving mathematical problems or playing tennis. Skills must be practiced to be retained or improved. Skills that are not practiced soon atrophy and become ineffective.

These skills can be used to promote healthy, self-enhancing behaviors as well as to overcome self-defeating behaviors. A necessity now is to review these skills and to plan to practice using them. An equally important point is to consider any additional steps you might need to take in order to promote your use of positive behaviors. Finally, you will be asked to think of events ahead of you that may pose difficult challenges as you attempt to behave productively and positively. The more prepared you are for challenges, the more likely you will behave in self-enhancing ways.

The purposes of Unit Six are

1. to review strategies for eliminating self-defeating behaviors;

2. to learn to use ESDB strategies for behaving in positive, self-enhancing ways;

3. to identify other sources of help as you develop new behaviors; and

4. to anticipate the challenges ahead and to prepare yourself for productive ways of handling them.

Reviewing the ESDB Strategies

Throughout this book, you have learned methods for exiting from the ESDB Circle using thoughts, actions, and feelings strategies. These methods included uncovering and disputing irrational thinking, developing more productive ways of thinking, acting in goal-oriented ways, making sure that your feelings are appropriate, calming yourself, and using your feelings as SDB cues. If you return to any of the preceding units, you will read once again how these strategies can be employed.

Remember that these strategies were developed because they help you exit from the self-defeating behavior circle. This circle shows how thoughts, actions, and feelings combine in complex ways to create and maintain SDBs. In the activity that follows, you will examine the SDB Circle again. This time, however, you will be collecting your thoughts regarding what you can do at each exit to break out of self-defeating behaviors.

Activity 6.1

REVIEWING THE SDB CIRCLE
AND ESDB STRATEGIES

Goals

1. To recall the ESDB strategies and

2. to relate them to the exits on the SDB Circle.

Directions

1. As you examine the SDB Circle below, recall at least one strategy that you can use to break-out of self-defeating behaviors at each of the exits. If you have difficulty recalling these strategies, refer back to Units Three, Four, and Five where they are described in detail.

2. Write those strategies from Step 1 on the lines below.

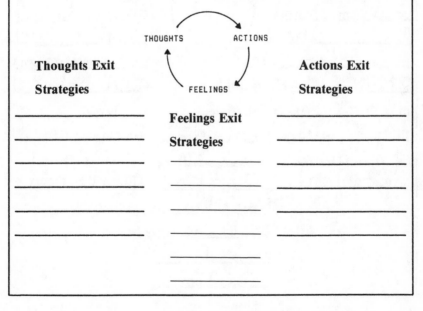

Thoughts Exit Strategies

_____
_____
_____
_____
_____
_____

Feelings Exit Strategies

_____
_____
_____
_____

Actions Exit Strategies

_____
_____
_____
_____
_____
_____

3. Use Step 2 as a "quick reference page."

By collecting the strategies here, you have created a "quick reference page" to which you can refer whenever you need help overcoming a self-defeating behavior. You may even want to make notes on this page as to where the details for each strategy are explained. This should truly facilitate your use of the ESDB System.

In the next section, you will consider how you can use these strategies to promote daily self-enhancing behaviors (SEBs) in yourself.

Kathy's Response

2. Write those strategies from Step 1 on the lines below.

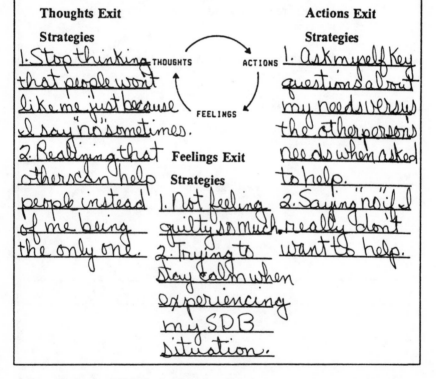

Thoughts Exit Strategies

1. Stop thinking that people won't like me just because I say "no" sometimes.

2. Realizing that others can help people instead of me being the only one.

Feelings Exit Strategies

1. Not feeling guilty so much.

2. Trying to stay calm when experiencing my SDB situation.

Actions Exit Strategies

1. Ask myself key questions about my needs versus the other persons needs when asked to help.

2. Saying "no" if I really don't want to help.

Mike's Response

2. Write those strategies from Step 1 on the lines below.

Thoughts Exit
Strategies

I will use THOUGHTS   ACTIONS

Actions Exit
Strategies

Rehearse what
Ellis' model to
check if my
thoughts are
rational

FEELINGS

I am going to
say before
actually dis-
cussing my
problems with
the boss.

Feelings Exit
Strategies

When I feel
the butterflies
I will
count-down
3 - 2 - 1.

ESDB Strategies for Self-Enhancing Behavior (SEB)

Many people, after learning these strategies, have come to a similar conclusion: the ESDB System can be used in daily living, whether you have self-defeating behaviors or not.

This suggests that these strategies, while developed to help people eliminate SDBs, also are useful as productive ways of living in general. In other words, you don't have to wait for a self-defeating behavior before you can use what you have learned in this book. You can use these methods in most of the situations you encounter each day. As you do, you will be thinking, acting, and feeling in appropriate and productive ways.

You learned, for example, that your basic beliefs about your environment and your opportunities affect your thoughts. In fact, these basic beliefs even affect the manner in which you seek information to confirm your thoughts about yourself. The more your basic beliefs allow you to think of yourself as in control, the more productive you will be and the better you will feel.

You have learned that effective goal setting and the use of an action plan allows you to be more task-oriented and purposeful. You will probably find that you can accomplish more while making more efficient use of your time as you become better at setting goals and minigoals. You also will give yourself more chances to feel relaxed, since you will know what is ahead of you next. Finally, goal setting gives you the opportunity to evaluate your own progress, thus freeing you from unnecessarily needing the evaluations of others.

You learned that feelings are sometimes blown out of proportion. While feeling emotions and physical sensations is important, just as important are those feelings that "fit" with the actual situation in which you are. You learned that you have a better chance to think clearly and act purposefully when your feelings are appropriate.

You can use these things you have learned about thoughts, actions, and feelings as guidelines for your future. The more often you can think, act, and feel in these positive, productive ways, the greater are the chances that you will enhance your life. You will be changing the SDB "D" to the SEB "E" as your behavior becomes more positive and productive.

Where Can You Turn for Help?

Many people build into their action plans at least one source of help that they will seek, such as psychological counseling, participation in support groups, or additional readings. This is a good point for you to consider what additional help you might need and where you can go for that assistance. While this book has given you new tools to use to help yourself, it cannot give you the individual attention nor the support that professional helpers can provide. While the contents of this book and the activities you did in proceeding through this book have given you some good information, many other books exist that can give you additional useful information.

You might consider talking with a close friend or family member about what you have accomplished and what you still hope to achieve. That conversation could lead to tips about other books or professionals that could help you while you are changing.

You could contact your state psychological association or consult the yellow pages of your telephone book to obtain the names of psychologists who practice in your area. Many psychologists specialize in behavior change techniques. Social workers, mental health counselors, and psychiatrists also can be valuable whenever you are trying to develop more effective ways of living.

Churches often sponsor discussion groups for adults and adolescents in which some of the topics covered in this book are explored. By attending these meetings, you could learn about sources of help in your community. You also could meet other people who are concerned about their personal development.

Colleges, universities, mental health centers, and libraries are additional resources upon which you could draw. Not only do these organizations have information, but also many employ professionals that could assist you. In addition, most offer adult education or continuing education programs that are designed to encourage personal development.

As you can see, many resources—people and places—exist to which you can turn for help. We urge you to take whatever steps you think will keep you moving toward the goal of enhancing yourself. The next activity will provide you with some structure for getting additional help.

Activity 6.2

ADDITIONAL HELP CHECK-OFF SHEET

Goal

To decide which community resources you could use as you continue your behavior change program.

Directions

1. Examine the community resources listed below and as you do so check those to which you could turn.

_____ Talking with a close friend
_____ Talking with a family member
_____ Talking with a teacher/instructor
_____ Calling the State Psychological Association (see the Yellow Pages under "Psychologists")
_____ Discussing your thoughts with a psychologist, social worker, mental health counselor, or psychiatrist
_____ Contacting churches to inquire about discussion groups
_____ Contacting a community college, university, or mental health center for information about continuing education classes
_____ Contacting the counseling service at a college, university, or mental health center
_____ Speaking with a librarian about personal development books or community lectures on personal development

2. Mark "1st" beside the one of those checked in Step 1 which you would use first if you need help immediately.

3. Now that you have noted which resources you could use, take the next step: contact one. Don't put this off; act now.

Kathy's Response

1. Examine the community resources listed below and as you do so check those to which you could turn.

1st X Talking with a close friend
___X___ Talking with a family member
_____ Talking with a teacher/instructor
_____ Calling the State Psychological Association (see the Yellow Pages under "Psychologists")
_____ Discussing your thoughts with a psychologist, social worker, mental health counselor, or psychiatrist
_____ Contacting churches to inquire about discussion groups
___X___ Contacting a community college, university, or mental health center for information about continuing education classes
_____ Contacting the counseling service at a college, university, or mental health center
___X___ Speaking with a librarian about personal development books or community lectures on personal development

2. Mark "1st" beside the one of those checked in Step 1 which you would use first if you need help immediately.

Mike's Response

1. Examine the community resources listed below and as you do so check those to which you could turn.

_____ Talking with a close friend
_____ Talking with a family member
__X__ Talking with a teacher/instructor
_____ Calling the State Psychological Association (see the Yellow Pages under "Psychologists")
__X__ Discussing your thoughts with a psychologist, social worker, mental health counselor, or psychiatrist
_____ Contacting churches to inquire about discussion groups
__X__ Contacting a community college, university, or mental health center for information about continuing education classes
1st __X__ Contacting the counseling service at a college, university, or mental health center
_____ Speaking with a librarian about personal development books or community lectures on personal development

2. Mark "1st" beside the one of those checked in Step 1 which you would use first if you need help immediately.

Handling the Challenges Ahead

Human beings seem to have a limited ability to predict the future. While you may be able to predict some of the challenges facing you, others will occur that you cannot anticipate today. In order to be successful at eliminating self-defeating behaviors (SDBs) and establishing self-enhancing behaviors (SEBs), you have to feel prepared to handle the upcoming challenges, whether they are predictable or not.

One challenge that you *can* predict is a resistance to change that comes from within you. As you attempt to use the strategies you learned for exiting the SDB Circle, you should expect to find yourself resisting change. Even though you may *want* to eliminate your self-defeating behaviors, you may find that doing so is more difficult than you anticipated. This is because people tend to resist change, even when change may be good for them.

The consequence of resisting change is the continued reliance on SDBs and the anxiety and unhappiness that accompanies them. To help relieve this anxiety and unhappiness people sometimes engage in behaviors that psychologists call "defense mechanisms." Some of the more common defense mechanisms are listed below.

1. **Rationalization.** This occurs when you try to explain an unacceptable behavior by believing in a more acceptable explanation. An example would be the following: You apply for a new job but are not accepted for it. You later tell yourself that you didn't really want the job.

2. **Projection.** When this occurs, you "project" onto someone else your own feelings or beliefs as if they belonged to the other person. An example would be accusing someone of being insensitive when you are the one displaying insensitivity.

3. **Regression.** You act or think in a childish manner when this occurs. An example would be the following: You demand something from another person. When the person refuses to go along with you, you scream and yell is if you were having a temper tantrum.

4. **Compensation.** When this occurs, you substitute a successful behavior to make up for repeated failures and unsuccessful

behaviors. An example would be the following: You have difficulty relating to others at work or in social situations. You
start to become excessively involved in an activity that allows
you to isolate yourself, such as long-distance running.

5. **Repression.** You push thoughts and memories that cause you
anxiety out of your consciousness when this occurs. An example would be forgetting the time you stole something, and
thus avoiding the associated guilt.

6. **Fantasy.** When this occurs, you engage in excessive
daydreaming as you imagine yourself experiencing success in
unrealistic situations. An example would be becoming lost in
thoughts as you dream that you will someday "strike it rich"
with a new invention.

Other defense mechanisms also exist, however the ones listed are the
ones frequently used. Also remember that most people use defense
mechanisms from time to time and their use can be quite normal.
However, if these mechanisms are used too frequently (i.e., excessively)
then this is a sign that you are denying reality. You also would be
avoiding behavioral changes that would benefit you. One challenge that
you can predict, consequently, is your potential to use defense
mechanisms in order to avoid behavioral change. You should try to
minimize your use of defense mechanisms.

As you have been tracking your SDB, you may have noticed that it
occurs more often when you are in particular places or with certain people. This type of information gives you the ability to predict future
challenges. You may be able to "count on yourself" to use your SDB
when the same situation occurs in the future or when you have to face the
same people. If you can "count on yourself" to fall back to old
behavioral habits, you can be even more prepared to use your ESDB
strategy when those situations or people appear. The chances will actually increase that you will avoid the SDB by being able to predict when it is
most likely to occur.

Yet, humans are not able to predict all future events. That reality
makes even more important your earnestly trying to behave in self-
enhancing ways. By doing so, you will be always ready to approach new
situations and people in a productive, positive manner. You also will
have far less to fear, since you will feel far more in control. Future events

will not block you nor cause you to lapse back to old behaviors if you view them as challenges for which the ESDB strategies can be successfully used.

Conclusion

In this unit you have reviewed the ESDB strategies, considered how they can be used daily to achieve self-enhancing behaviors (SEBs), identified other sources of help as you continue your attempts to change, and considered how you can prepare yourself for future challenges.

As you work toward positive, productive approaches to life experiences, this book can serve as a reminder of all the power you have to guide and control yourself and your reactions to others. You may find that you will refer to it often, seeking tips about the strategies that work best for you. You also will find that your belief in your own power to control your life is a major key in making the ESDB System work for you.

REFERENCES

Cerio, J.E. (1983). The use of hypnotic elements and audio recordings with the fantasy relaxation technique. *Personnel and Guidance Journal, 61,* 436-7.

Cronkhite, G. (1976). *Communication and awareness.* Menlo Park, CA: Cummings.

Cudney, M.R. (1975). *Eliminating self-defeating behaviors.* Kalamazoo, MI: Life Giving Enterprises.

Ellis, A. (1977). The basic clinical theory of rational-emotive therapy. In A. Ellis & R. Grieger (Eds.), *Handbook of rational-emotive therapy.* New York: Springer.

Ellis, A., & Grieger, R. (Eds.). (1977). *Handbook of rational-emotive therapy.* New York: Springer.

Ellis, A., & Harper, R.A. (1975). *A new guide to rational living.* No. Hollywood, CA: Wilshire.

Frank, J. (1974). *Persuasion and healing.* New York: Schocken.

Glasser, W. (1975). *Reality therapy.* New York: Harper & Row.

Gunnison, H. (1976). Fantasy relaxation technique. *Personnel and Guidance Journal, 55,* 199-200.

Meichenbaum, D. (1977). *Cognitive-behavior modification: An integrative approach.* New York: Plenum.

Meichenbaum, D. (1985). *Stress inoculation training.* New York: Pergamon.

Ohlsen, M.M. (1977). *Group counseling (2nd ed.).* New York: Holt, Rinehart & Winston.

Ohlsen, M.M. (1983). *Introduction to counseling.* Itasca, IL: F.E. Peacock.

James E. Cerio, Associate Professor of Counseling and Psychology at Harford Community College, is a psychologist, college counselor, psychology instructor, and private practitioner in Bel Air, Maryland. His Ph.D. in counseling psychology is from Indiana State University in Terre Haute, and his psychology internship was completed at Counseling and Psychological Services, Indiana University, Bloomington.

Dr. Cerio uses cognitive-behavioral approaches in individual and couples counseling, workshops, training programs, and consultations. He assists adults and adolescents with anxiety, adjustment, affective, identity, and personality disorders. His work also includes psychological evaluations, career and developmental counseling, and marriage counseling. He teaches General Psychology, Educational Psychology, and Eliminating Self-Defeating Behaviors, and he conducts training workshops in short-term cognitive-behavioral counseling and initial assessments.

Dr. Cerio has published papers in *The Personnel and Guidance Journal, Journal for Specialists in Group Work,* and *Contemporary Education.* He has presented programs at meetings of the American College Personnel Association and the American Association for Counseling and Development. He is a Registrant in the National Register of Health Service Providers in Psychology and a member of the American Psychological Association and Maryland Psychological Association.

James F. LaCalle, Associate Dean for Continuing Education at Harford Community College, Bel Air, Maryland, is an administrator primarily concerned with developing continuing education programs for adults. He also teaches psychology and business courses, including training courses for business and industry.

Dr. LaCalle's master's degree in guidance and counseling was completed at The Johns Hopkins University in Baltimore, Maryland, and his doctoral degree in Higher Education Administration was received from The American University in Washington, D.C. He has completed the Harvard University Institute for the Management of Lifelong Learning.

Dr. LaCalle is active in a number of professional associations, having served as Chairman of the Maryland Association of Deans and Directors of Continuing Education and Community Services. He also has been an officer in the Maryland Association for Adult, Community, and Continuing Education, serving as President for the 1986-87 program year.

James P. Murtha

James P. Murtha is the Associate Dean of the Human Development Division at Harford Community College in Bel Air, Maryland. He is an academic administrator with professional responsibilities for a number of programs and services related to the Behavioral Sciences and is a member of the psychology faculty as well. His Ph.D. is in higher education administration from The Catholic University of America, and he completed a management development program for college and university administrators at the Harvard University Institute for Educational Management.

Dr. Murtha's master's degree is in Counseling and Guidance from the University of Alabama, and he served as Director of the Counseling Center at Harford Community College for many years. He continues to have administrative responsibilities for the comprehensive counseling programs at that college.

Dr. Murtha teaches courses in Human Relations and Group Dynamics. He consults with a variety of organizations, conducting workshops and seminars focusing on management and supervision.